The Pillsbury
Family
Christmas Cookbook

Pictured clockwise from upper left: Taffy, page 43; Jolly Santa Lollipops, page 95; Easy Chocolate Truffles, page 39; Candy Cane Cookies, page 20; Cran-Apple Spiced Jelly, page 59; Molasses Ginger Cutouts, page 9.

The Pillsbury
Family
Christmas
Cookbook

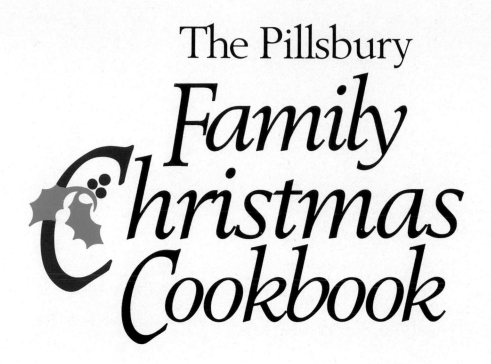

DOUBLEDAY
New York • London • Toronto • Sydney • Auckland

The Pillsbury Company
Pillsbury Publications, Publisher of Pillsbury Classic® Cookbooks

Publisher: Sally Peters
Publication Manager: Diane B. Anderson
Associate Editor: Elaine Christiansen
Senior Food Editor: Jackie Sheehan
Test Kitchen Coordinator: Pat Peterson
Recipe Copy Editor: Nancy A. Lilleberg
Contributing Editor: Patricia Miller
Home Economists: Pillsbury Publications
Nutrition Coordinators: Patricia Godfrey, R.D., Indra Mehrotra, R.D.,
    Diane Christensen
Art Direction and Design: Tad Ware & Company, Inc.
Photography: Studio 3
Food Stylists: JoAnn Cherry, Sharon Harding, Barb Standal
Book Editor: Karen Van Westering
Front Cover Photograph: Partridge Bread with Orange-Honey Butter,
page 46

PUBLISHED BY DOUBLEDAY
a division of Bantam Doubleday Dell Publishing Group, Inc.
666 Fifth Avenue, New York, New York 10103
DOUBLEDAY and the portrayal of an anchor with a dolphin
are trademarks of Doubleday, a division of Bantam Doubleday Dell
Publishing Group, Inc.

Library of Congress Cataloging-in-Publication Data
The Pillsbury family Christmas cookbook—1st ed.
    p.   cm.
    Includes index.
    1. Christmas cookery.   I. Pillsbury Company.
TX739.2.C45P55   1991
641.5′68—dc20   90-23885
ISBN 0-385-23866-5   CIP

Contents

Celebrate with Cookies

A Christmas Collection of Cookies & Bars

The day comes, somewhere between Halloween and Christmas itself, when the air is spicy crisp, the trees etch black shadows on new-fallen snow and the very house seems to whisper, "Christmas is coming." That's the day when you say, "Let's bake cookies."

Cookie baking ushers in this most festive of seasons for many families, an activity that becomes a treasured memory long after the cookies have been enjoyed. Bake bountiful batches for happy gatherings from caroling parties to pageants to open houses to Christmas Eve dinner. Bake them as gifts for friends and teachers, as offerings at bazaars, as activities for Scout troops.

Home economists in the Pillsbury Kitchens collected a seasonful of cookies and bars for your holiday celebrations. Some, like Springerle and Candied Fruit Squares, are right out of Grandma's recipe box. Others take on holiday forms: Candy Cane Cookies, Jingle Bells, Linzer Stars and O Christmas Tree Cookies.

For Christmas cookie baking that's almost too easy to believe, try our Holiday Cookie Mix. It's a butter cookie mix that stores in the refrigerator or freezer for up to four weeks. Transform it into a baker's dozen of dazzling cookies and bars, including Chocolate-Dipped Orange Supremes, Molasses Ginger Cutouts, Pumpkin-Raisin Drops and Coconut Cherry Chews.

Cookies can relieve some of the pressure of holiday preparations, since many can be made days or even weeks ahead and stored in tins or in the freezer. In fact, cookies made with butter will actually taste richer when given a chance to mellow in tightly covered tins or cookie jars.

When sending cookies afar, choose ones that travel well, such as drop cookies or unfrosted bars. Good travelers in this collection include Apricot-Raisin Bars, English Toffee Balls and Chocolate-Orange Pinwheels.

And when creating a cookie sampler, to give or for the family to enjoy, remember to combine shapes, flavors, sizes and colors for an assortment that's as lovely to look at as it is delicious to eat.

Easy does it in the cookie-making department with an opportunity to fashion a baker's dozen from one simple mix. You will be amazed at the variety displayed in the recipes on the following five pages, all of which feature the Holiday Cookie Mix. Add a personal touch to this sampling with your own creative decorating ideas. It is a quick and easy way to create a cookie sampler for family and friends.

Holiday Cookie Mix

12 cups all purpose or unbleached flour
7 cups sugar
2 tablespoons baking powder
4 teaspoons salt
4 cups (2 pounds) margarine or butter

Lightly spoon flour into measuring cup; level off. In 4-quart bowl or container, combine ½ each of the flour, sugar, baking powder and salt. Using fork or pastry blender, cut ½ of the margarine into flour mixture until mixture resembles coarse crumbs. Place in large, tightly covered container. Repeat with remaining half of ingredients. Store in refrigerator or freezer. Use within 4 weeks. Measure by dipping cup into mix; level off. Return unused mix to refrigerator or freezer. *Allow measured mix to come to room temperature* before adding ingredients to make any of the recipes in this collection.
22 to 23 cups cookie mix.

TIPS: To prepare cookie mix in food processor, place ¼ of each ingredient in food processor bowl with metal blade. Process until mixture resembles coarse crumbs. Place in tightly covered container. Repeat with remaining ingredients.

If desired, recipe can be cut in half. Prepare mix as directed above. 11 to 12 cups cookie mix.

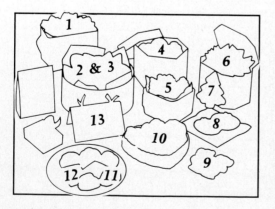

Chocolate-Dipped Orange Supremes

COOKIES
4 cups Holiday Cookie Mix
4 teaspoons milk
2 teaspoons grated orange peel
1 teaspoon vanilla
1 egg

GLAZE
6 ounces (6 squares) semi-sweet chocolate, cut into pieces
4 teaspoons shortening

Dip measuring cup into mix and level off; allow to come to room temperature. In large bowl, combine all cookie ingredients at low speed until well mixed and dough forms. Divide dough in half; place each half on sheet of waxed paper. Shape each half into a log 1 inch in diameter. Wrap in waxed paper; refrigerate ½ hour. Remove logs from refrigerator. For oval cookies, mold logs into an oval shape. For triangular cookies, mold logs into a triangular shape. Rewrap; refrigerate until firm, about 3 hours.

Heat oven to 375°F. Cut dough into ¼-inch slices. Place 1 inch apart on ungreased cookie sheets. Bake at 375°F. for 6 to 10 minutes or until edges are light golden brown. Cool completely.

In small saucepan over low heat, melt chocolate and shortening, stirring constantly. Set saucepan in hot water to maintain dipping consistency. Dip ends of cooled cookies into chocolate mixture; allow excess to drip off. Place cookies on sheet of waxed paper. Allow glaze to set. Store between sheets of waxed paper in loosely covered container in a cool place.

8 dozen cookies.

HIGH ALTITUDE – Above 3500 Feet: Add ¼ cup flour to the 4 cups Holiday Cookie Mix. Bake as directed above.

NUTRITION INFORMATION PER SERVING

Serving Size: 1 cookie		Percent U.S. RDA	
Calories	40	Protein	*
Protein	0g	Vitamin A	*
Carbohydrate	5g	Vitamin C	*
Fat	2g	Thiamine	*
Cholesterol	2mg	Riboflavin	*
Sodium	30mg	Niacin	*
Potassium	10mg	Calcium	*
		Iron	*
		*Contains less than 2%	

Molasses Ginger Cutouts

4 cups Holiday Cookie Mix
2 teaspoons ginger
¼ cup molasses
1 egg

Dip measuring cup into mix and level off; allow to come to room temperature. Heat oven to 350°F. In large bowl, combine all ingredients at low speed until well mixed and dough forms. If necessary, refrigerate dough 1 hour for easier handling. On well-floured surface, roll out ⅓ of dough at a time to ¼-inch thickness. (Refrigerate remaining dough.) Cut with floured cookie cutters. Place 1 inch apart on ungreased cookie sheets. Bake at 350°F. for 10 to 15 minutes or until set. Cool 1 minute; remove from cookie sheets. Decorate as desired.

3½ dozen cookies.

HIGH ALTITUDE – Above 3500 Feet: Add 4 tablespoons flour to the 4 cups cookie mix.

TIP: For teddy bear shaped cookies, see Silhouette Cookies, page 10, for shaping; decorate with heart cut from tinted Crispy Sugar Cookie dough.

NUTRITION INFORMATION PER SERVING

Serving Size: 1		Percent U.S. RDA	
Molasses Ginger		Protein	*
Cutout cookie		Vitamin A	2%
Calories	70	Vitamin C	*
Protein	1g	Thiamine	2%
Carbohydrate	11g	Riboflavin	2%
Fat	3g	Niacin	*
Cholesterol	5mg	Calcium	*
Sodium	70mg	Iron	2%
Potassium	30mg	*Contains less than 2%	

Gift Suggestions

For Cookie Enthusiasts

Cookie stamp
Springerle pin or mold
Cookie press
Assortment of cookie cutters
Canapé cutters for bite-size cookies
Christmas plate or tray for serving cookies
Decorative tins, boxes or bags to store cookies
Colored or patterned tissue for lining cookie containers
Decorating bag and tips
Mixing bowl set
Cookie sheets
Measuring spoons and cups
Rolling pin, stockinette and pastry cloth

Crispy Sugar Cookies

4 cups Holiday Cookie Mix
2 tablespoons milk
1 teaspoon vanilla
1 egg

Dip measuring cup into mix and level off; allow to come to room temperature. Heat oven to 350°F. In large bowl, combine all ingredients at low speed until well mixed and soft dough forms. If necessary, refrigerate dough 1 hour for easier handling.

On well-floured surface, roll out ⅓ of dough at a time to ¼-inch thickness; cut with floured 2-inch cookie cutter. Place 1 inch apart on ungreased cookie sheets. Bake at 350°F. for 12 to 16 minutes or until edges are light golden brown. Cool 1 minute; remove from cookie sheets. Decorate as desired.
3½ dozen cookies.

HIGH ALTITUDE – Above 3500 Feet: Add 4 tablespoons flour to the 4 cups Cookie Mix.

VARIATIONS:

CHRISTMAS CARD COOKIES: Prepare cookie dough as directed above. On well-floured surface, roll out ⅓ of dough at a time to ¼-inch thickness. With sharp knife, cut dough into 5 × 3-inch rectangles. Place on ungreased cookie sheets. Paint desired design and holiday message on unbaked cookies, using directions for Painted Cookies (below). Punch holes with drinking straw in top or on 1 side of each rectangle. Bake as directed above. Tie cookies together with colored ribbon or yarn.

SILHOUETTE COOKIES: Prepare cookie dough as directed above and divide in half. Color each portion with a different food color. On floured surface, roll out each portion of dough; cut with floured cookie cutter. Place 1 inch apart on ungreased cookie sheets. Using small canapé cutter, cut out cen-

ter of each cookie and replace with center of opposite color. Bake as directed above.

PAINTED COOKIES: Prepare cookie dough and cut out as directed above. Place on ungreased cookie sheets. Divide ¾ cup evaporated milk into small bowls; tint each with a different food color. Using small paintbrush and colored milk, paint desired designs on unbaked cookies. Bake as directed above.

NUTRITION INFORMATION PER SERVING

Serving Size: 1 Crispy Sugar Cookie		Percent U.S. RDA	
Calories	70	Protein	*
		Vitamin A	2%
Protein	1g	Vitamin C	*
Carbohydrate	9g	Thiamine	2%
Fat	3g	Riboflavin	2%
Cholesterol	5mg	Niacin	*
Sodium	70mg	Calcium	*
Potassium	10mg	Iron	*
		*Contains less than 2%	

Peanut Butter Chocolate Stars

3 cups Holiday Cookie Mix
½ cup peanut butter
1 teaspoon vanilla
1 egg
Milk chocolate stars

Dip measuring cup into mix and level off; allow to come to room temperature. Heat oven to 375°F. In large bowl, combine mix, peanut butter, vanilla and egg at low speed until well mixed and dough forms. Shape dough into 1-inch balls. Place 2 inches apart on ungreased cookie sheets. Bake at 375°F. for 10 to 15 minutes or until edges are light golden brown. Immediately place 1 chocolate star in center of each cookie, pressing down lightly. Remove from cookie sheets; cool completely.
3 dozen cookies.

HIGH ALTITUDE – Above 3500 Feet: No change.

NUTRITION INFORMATION PER SERVING

Serving Size: 1 cookie		Percent U.S. RDA	
Calories	100	Protein	2%
Protein	2g	Vitamin A	2%
Carbohydrate	12g	Vitamin C	*
Fat	6g	Thiamine	2%
Cholesterol	6mg	Riboflavin	2%
Sodium	85mg	Niacin	4%
Potassium	55mg	Calcium	*
		Iron	2%
		*Contains less than 2%	

COOK'S NOTE

Cutout Cookie Tips

• Dough should be stiff and moist enough to roll easily (but not so stiff that it breaks apart). Therefore, measure ingredients accurately to get the best possible consistency.

• When a cookie dough is soft, the recipe directions often include chilling time to firm the dough.

• Work with a small amount of dough at a time, keeping any remaining portion covered to avoid drying, and refrigerate if necessary to retain firmness.

• Roll out dough on a lightly floured surface. A rolling pin with a non-stick surface or a stockinette covering helps the process.

• For tender cookies, roll out and handle dough as little as possible.

• Follow recipe directions for cookie sheet preparation and placement of cookies on pan to avoid sticking and to preserve shapes.

• Cool cookie sheets between bakes to keep dough from spreading.

• Remove baked cookies from hot cookie sheets according to instructions, using a wide metal spatula for support.

Pictured clockwise from upper left: Peanut Butter Chocolate Stars; Silhouette Cookies; Painted Cookies; Fast 'n Festive Pressed Cookies

Fast 'n Festive Pressed Cookies

3 cups Holiday Cookie Mix
⅓ cup dairy sour cream
Colored sugar, if desired

Dip measuring cup into mix and level off; allow to come to room temperature. Heat oven to 375°F. In large bowl, combine mix and sour cream at low speed until well mixed and dough forms. Fill cookie press; press dough in desired shapes onto ungreased cookie sheets. Sprinkle with colored sugar.

Bake at 375°F. for 8 to 11 minutes or until edges are light golden brown. Cool 1 minute; remove from cookie sheets. **3½ dozen cookies.**

HIGH ALTITUDE – Above 3500 Feet: Add 4 tablespoons flour to the 3 cups cookie mix.

NUTRITION INFORMATION PER SERVING

Serving Size: 1 cookie		Percent U.S. RDA	
Calories	50	Protein	*
Protein	1g	Vitamin A	*
Carbohydrate	8g	Vitamin C	*
Fat	2g	Thiamine	2%
Cholesterol	1mg	Riboflavin	*
Sodium	55mg	Niacin	*
Potassium	10mg	Calcium	*
		Iron	*
		*Contains less than 2%	

Chocolate-Orange Pinwheels

4 cups Holiday Cookie Mix
2 tablespoons milk
1 teaspoon vanilla
1 egg
2 tablespoons unsweetened cocoa
2 teaspoons grated orange peel

Dip measuring cup into mix and level off; allow to come to room temperature. In large bowl, combine mix, milk, vanilla and egg at low speed until well mixed and dough forms.* Divide dough in half. Blend cocoa into half the dough; blend orange peel into remaining half. Roll out each half of dough between sheets of waxed paper to 12 × 7-inch rectangle. Remove waxed paper from tops of dough; invert and place chocolate dough over orange dough, pressing lightly to seal. Remove top waxed paper. Starting with longer side, roll up jelly-roll fashion using waxed paper as guide. Wrap roll in waxed paper; refrigerate at least 2 hours or overnight.

Heat oven to 350°F. Cut dough into ¼-inch slices. Place 1 inch apart on ungreased cookie sheets. Bake at 350°F. for 11 to 15 minutes or until edges are light golden brown.
4 dozen cookies.

TIP: *If dough seems dry, add milk 1 teaspoon at a time until dough is of rolling consistency.

HIGH ALTITUDE — Above 3500 Feet: Add 4 tablespoons flour with orange peel to orange dough.

NUTRITION INFORMATION PER SERVING

Serving Size: 1 cookie		Percent U.S. RDA	
Calories	60	Protein	*
Protein	1g	Vitamin A	2%
Carbohydrate	8g	Vitamin C	*
Fat	3g	Thiamine	2%
Cholesterol	4mg	Riboflavin	*
Sodium	65mg	Niacin	*
Potassium	10mg	Calcium	*
		Iron	*
		*Contains less than 2%	

Candied Fruit Squares

BASE
3 cups Holiday Cookie Mix
1 egg

FILLING
1 (16-ounce) package (2 cups) diced mixed candied fruit
1 cup chopped dates
1 cup coconut
1 cup chopped nuts
1 (14-ounce) can sweetened condensed milk (not evaporated)

Dip measuring cup into mix and level off; allow to come to room temperature. Heat oven to 350°F. In large bowl, combine mix and egg at low speed until well mixed. (Mixture will be crumbly.) Press into ungreased 15 × 10 × 1-inch baking pan.

In large bowl, combine all filling ingredients; carefully spread over base. Bake at 350°F. for 25 to 35 minutes or until light golden brown. Cool completely; cut into bars.
54 bars.

HIGH ALTITUDE — Above 3500 Feet: No change.

NUTRITION INFORMATION PER SERVING

Serving Size: 1 bar		Percent U.S. RDA	
Calories	130	Protein	2%
Protein	2g	Vitamin A	2%
Carbohydrate	21g	Vitamin C	*
Fat	4g	Thiamine	2%
Cholesterol	7mg	Riboflavin	4%
Sodium	80mg	Niacin	*
Potassium	90mg	Calcium	4%
		Iron	2%
		*Contains less than 2%	

Pumpkin-Raisin Drops

4 cups Holiday Cookie Mix
1 cup canned pumpkin
1½ teaspoons cinnamon
½ teaspoon nutmeg
1 egg
1 cup raisins
½ cup chopped nuts
1 can ready-to-spread cream cheese frosting
Nutmeg

COOK'S NOTE

Storing Cookies

To get a step ahead of the holidays, remember that most *unbaked* cookie dough can be frozen up to a year when properly wrapped in an airtight, moistureproof wrap. Also, most *baked* cookies freeze well and can be kept frozen for three to six months. After the baked cookies have thoroughly cooled, layer them in a container and then wrap, seal, label and freeze. For the best flavor and appearance, postpone frosting and decorating the cookies until they are removed from the freezer.

Dip measuring cup into mix and level off; allow to come to room temperature. Heat oven to 350°F. Lightly grease cookie sheets. In large bowl, combine mix, pumpkin, cinnamon, nutmeg and egg at low speed until well mixed and soft dough forms. Stir in raisins and nuts. Drop by rounded teaspoonfuls 2 inches apart onto greased cookie sheets. Bake at 350°F. for 12 to 17 minutes or until set. Remove from cookie sheets; cool completely. Frost cooled cookies; sprinkle with nutmeg. Cover any remaining frosting and refrigerate.

4 dozen cookies.

HIGH ALTITUDE—Above 3500 Feet: Add 2 tablespoons flour to the 4 cups cookie mix. Bake as directed above.

NUTRITION INFORMATION PER SERVING

Serving Size: 1 cookie		Percent U.S. RDA	
Calories	120	Protein	*
Protein	1g	Vitamin A	25%
Carbohydrate	18g	Vitamin C	*
Fat	5g	Thiamine	2%
Cholesterol	4mg	Riboflavin	2%
Sodium	80mg	Niacin	*
Potassium	50mg	Calcium	*
		Iron	2%
		*Contains less than 2%	

Chocolate-Mint Brownies

2 cups Holiday Cookie Mix
1 (6-ounce) package (1 cup) semi-sweet chocolate chips
½ cup chopped nuts
1 teaspoon vanilla
2 eggs
16 creme-filled chocolate mints

Dip measuring cup into mix and level off; allow to come to room temperature. Heat oven to 350°F. Grease 9-inch square pan. In small saucepan over low heat, melt chocolate chips, stirring constantly. In large bowl, combine mix, melted chocolate chips, nuts, vanilla and eggs at low speed just until blended. Spread evenly in greased pan.

Bake at 350°F. for 20 to 25 minutes or until set. Immediately arrange mints on top; return to oven and bake an addi-

tional 5 minutes. Spread softened mints evenly over brownie surface. Cool completely; cut into bars.

24 bars.

HIGH ALTITUDE—Above 3500 Feet: No change.

NUTRITION INFORMATION PER SERVING

Serving Size: 1 bar		Percent U.S. RDA	
Calories	140	Protein	2%
Protein	2g	Vitamin A	2%
Carbohydrate	16g	Vitamin C	*
Fat	8g	Thiamine	2%
Cholesterol	18mg	Riboflavin	2%
Sodium	75mg	Niacin	*
Potassium	55mg	Calcium	*
		Iron	2%
		*Contains less than 2%	

Coconut-Cherry Chews

3 cups Holiday Cookie Mix
1 cup coconut
2 teaspoons almond extract
1 egg
1 egg white
1 tablespoon water
1 to 1½ cups coconut
Red candied cherries, halved

Dip measuring cup into mix and level off; allow to come to room temperature. Heat oven to 375°F. Grease cookie sheets. In large bowl, combine mix, 1 cup coconut, almond extract and egg at low speed until well mixed and dough forms. In small bowl, beat egg white and water until foamy. Shape dough into 1-inch balls. Dip in egg white mixture; roll in coconut. Place 2 inches apart on greased cookie sheets. Place cherry in center of each cookie, pressing down lightly. Bake at 375°F. for 11 to 14 minutes or until edges are light golden brown.

3 dozen cookies.

HIGH ALTITUDE—Above 3500 Feet: No change.

NUTRITION INFORMATION PER SERVING

Serving Size: 1 cookie		Percent U.S. RDA	
Calories	90	Protein	*
Protein	1g	Vitamin A	2%
Carbohydrate	12g	Vitamin C	*
Fat	5g	Thiamine	2%
Cholesterol	6mg	Riboflavin	2%
Sodium	65mg	Niacin	*
Potassium	35mg	Calcium	*
		Iron	2%
		*Contains less than 2%	

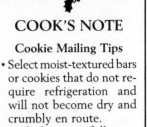

COOK'S NOTE

Cookie Mailing Tips

• Select moist-textured bars or cookies that do not require refrigeration and will not become dry and crumbly en route.
• Pack them carefully in a sturdy corrugated carton.
• Cushion layers of cookies with waxed paper.
• Seal the carton tightly.
• Mark your package PERISHABLE and send it the most expedient way.

Linzer Stars

Linzer Stars

½ cup sugar
½ cup butter or margarine, softened
1 tablespoon milk
1 teaspoon vanilla
1 egg
1¼ cups all purpose or unbleached
   flour
1 teaspoon cream of tartar
½ teaspoon baking soda
¼ teaspoon salt
   Powdered sugar
½ cup cherry or red currant jelly

In large bowl, beat sugar and butter until light and fluffy. Add milk, vanilla and egg; blend well. Lightly spoon flour into measuring cup; level off. Stir in flour, cream of tartar, baking soda and salt; mix well. Cover with plastic wrap; refrigerate 3 hours for easier handling.

Heat oven to 425°F. Using stockinette-covered rolling pin and well-floured pastry cloth, roll out ⅓ of dough at a time to ⅛-inch thickness. (Refrigerate remaining dough.) Cut with floured 3-inch star-shaped cookie cutter.* Using 1-inch round cookie cutter, cut out center of half of dough stars to form cookie tops. Place stars 1 inch apart on ungreased cookie sheets. Repeat with remaining dough. Bake at 425°F. for 3 to 5 minutes or until edges are light golden brown. Cool 1 minute; remove from cookie sheets. Cool completely.

To assemble cookies, sprinkle powdered sugar over cookie tops. Spread ½ teaspoon jelly over each cookie bottom. Place sugar-topped cookie over jelly. **4 dozen sandwich cookies.**

TIP: *A 2½-inch round cookie cutter can be substituted for star-shaped cutter.

HIGH ALTITUDE—Above 3500 Feet: Increase flour to 1¼ cups plus 2 tablespoons. Bake as directed above.

NUTRITION INFORMATION PER SERVING

Serving Size: 1 sandwich cookie		Percent U.S. RDA	
Calories	50	Protein	*
Protein	1g	Vitamin A	*
Carbohydrate	7g	Vitamin C	*
Fat	2g	Thiamine	*
Cholesterol	10mg	Riboflavin	*
Sodium	45mg	Niacin	*
Potassium	10mg	Calcium	*
		Iron	*
		*Contains less than 2%	

COOK'S NOTE

Butter, Margarine or Shortening?

Butter or quality margarine gives good flavor and a crisp texture to cookies. Vegetable shortening provides little flavor and produces a more crumbly cookie. Diet or whipped margarines are not recommended for baking because their lower fat content gives variable, unsatisfactory results.

Grandma's Date-Filled Cookies

COOKIES
1½ cups firmly packed brown sugar
1 cup margarine or butter, softened
1 teaspoon vanilla
3 eggs
3½ cups all purpose or unbleached flour
1 teaspoon baking soda

FILLING
2 cups chopped dates
1 cup sugar
1 cup water

In large bowl, beat brown sugar and margarine until light and fluffy. Add vanilla and eggs; beat well. Lightly spoon flour into measuring cup; level off. Stir in flour and baking soda; mix well. Cover with plastic wrap; refrigerate at least 2 hours for easier handling.

Meanwhile, in medium saucepan combine all filling ingredients. Bring to a boil; reduce heat and simmer 10 minutes, stirring frequently. Refrigerate until ready to use. (Mixture will thicken as it cools.)

Heat oven to 375°F. On well-floured surface, roll out ⅓ of dough at a time to ⅛-inch thickness. (Refrigerate remaining dough.) Cut with floured 2½-inch round cookie cutter. Place half of dough rounds on ungreased cookie sheet; spoon 1 teaspoon cooled filling onto each. In remaining half of dough rounds, cut and remove 1-inch round hole in center to form dough rings.* Place dough rings over filling-topped dough rounds on cookie sheet. Using fingertips or fork, press outside edge of dough to seal. Repeat with remaining dough and filling. Bake at 375°F. for 7 to 10 minutes or until light golden brown.
3½ dozen cookies.

TIP: *A 2½-inch doughnut cutter can be used to make the dough rings.

HIGH ALTITUDE — Above 3500 Feet: No change.

NUTRITION INFORMATION PER SERVING

Serving Size: 1 cookie		Percent U.S. RDA	
Calories	150	Protein	2%
Protein	2g	Vitamin A	4%
Carbohydrate	27g	Vitamin C	*
Fat	5g	Thiamine	6%
Cholesterol	15mg	Riboflavin	4%
Sodium	90mg	Niacin	4%
Potassium	100mg	Calcium	*
		Iron	4%
*Contains less than 2%			

English Toffee Balls

½ cup powdered sugar
1 cup margarine or butter, softened
1 (3½-ounce) package instant vanilla pudding and pie filling mix
2 cups all purpose or unbleached flour
1 tablespoon milk
1 teaspoon vanilla
3 (¾-ounce) chocolate-coated English toffee bars, crushed
Powdered sugar

Heat oven to 325°F. In large bowl, beat powdered sugar, margarine and pudding mix until light and fluffy. Lightly spoon flour into measuring cup; level off. Add flour, milk, vanilla and crushed toffee bars; mix well. Shape dough into 1-inch balls. Place on ungreased cookie sheets. Bake at 325°F. for 13 to 18 minutes or until edges are light golden brown. Remove from cookie sheets; cool completely. Dip top of each cookie into powdered sugar.
6 dozen cookies.

HIGH ALTITUDE — Above 3500 Feet: No change.

NUTRITION INFORMATION PER SERVING

Serving Size: 1 cookie		Percent U.S. RDA	
Calories	50	Protein	*
Protein	0g	Vitamin A	2%
Carbohydrate	5g	Vitamin C	*
Fat	3g	Thiamine	2%
Cholesterol	0mg	Riboflavin	*
Sodium	40mg	Niacin	*
Potassium	10mg	Calcium	*
		Iron	*
*Contains less than 2%			

Grandma's Date-Filled Cookies

A soft brown sugar cookie with a delicious date filling. For variety, use other cookie cutter shapes such as hearts or diamonds.

English Toffee Balls

English toffee candy bars add a special flavor and texture.

Meringue Mushrooms

Meringue Mushrooms

Serve these delicate bite-size mushrooms as cookies or use them to decorate our Yule Log Cake (see page 71). The recipe variation, Mint Wreaths, will melt in your mouth!

Starlight Bites

The buttery filling in these delicate cookies makes them almost melt in your mouth.

2 egg whites
¼ teaspoon cream of tartar
½ cup sugar
  Unsweetened cocoa
2 ounces (2 squares) semi-sweet
  chocolate

Heat oven to 200°F. Cover 2 cookie sheets with foil or parchment paper. In small bowl, beat egg whites and cream of tartar until foamy. Beat in sugar 1 tablespoon at a time; continue beating until meringue is stiff and glossy. Spoon meringue into decorating bag with ¼-inch plain decorating tip (No. 10, 11 or 12). For mushroom caps, pipe about fifty 1-inch mounds on 1 foil-lined cookie sheet. Lightly sift cocoa over caps. Bake at 200°F. for 45 to 60 minutes or until firm and very lightly browned. Remove from oven. Immediately turn caps over; with finger, make indentation in center of each cap. Cool completely. Brush off any excess cocoa.

Meanwhile, pipe remaining meringue into 50 upright stems, about ¾ inch tall, on second foil-lined cookie sheet. Bake at 200°F. for 40 to 45 minutes or until firm. Immediately remove from cookie sheet; cool completely.

Melt chocolate in small saucepan over low heat, stirring constantly. To assemble each mushroom, spread a small amount of melted chocolate in indentation of cap; insert pointed end of stem into chocolate. Let stand until dry. Store loosely covered at room temperature.
4 to 5 dozen cookies.

NUTRITION INFORMATION PER SERVING

Serving Size: 1 Meringue Mushroom		Percent U.S. RDA	
		Protein	*
Calories	12	Vitamin A	*
Protein	0g	Vitamin C	*
Carbohydrate	2g	Thiamine	*
Fat	0g	Riboflavin	*
Cholesterol	0mg	Niacin	*
Sodium	0mg	Calcium	*
Potassium	5mg	Iron	*
		*Contains less than 2%	

VARIATION:

MINT WREATHS: *Omit cocoa and chocolate.* Add ¼ teaspoon mint extract and a few drops of green food color, if desired, to egg whites when adding last tablespoon of sugar. Spoon meringue into decorating bag with ¼-inch plain decorating tip. Pipe two 1½-inch circles of meringue, one on top of the other, on foil-lined cookie sheet. Decorate with bits of red and green candied cherries. Bake at 200°F. for 45 minutes. Turn oven off; leave meringues in oven an additional 1 hour to dry. Carefully peel from foil. Cool completely.
3 dozen cookies.

Starlight Bites

COOKIES
2 cups all purpose or unbleached
  flour
1 cup butter or margarine, softened
⅓ cup whipping cream
¼ cup sugar

FILLING
¼ cup butter or margarine, softened
1 cup powdered sugar
1 teaspoon vanilla
  Whipping cream
  Red and green food color

Lightly spoon flour into measuring cup; level off. In medium bowl, combine flour, 1 cup butter and ⅓ cup whipping cream; mix well. Cover with plastic wrap; refrigerate 1 to 2 hours for easier handling.

Heat oven to 375°F. Place sugar in small bowl. On floured surface, roll out half of dough to ⅛-inch thickness. (Refrigerate remaining dough.) With floured 1½-inch round cutter, cut circles. Coat both sides of each circle with sugar. Place 1 inch apart on ungreased cookie sheets. With fork, prick each circle 3 or 4 times. Bake at 375°F. for 7 to 9 minutes or until slightly puffy but not brown. Remove from cookie sheets; cool completely.

Mint Wreaths; Starlight Bites; Three-Tiered Trees, page 18

Roll out remaining dough to ⅛-inch thickness. With floured 1-inch star cutter, cut the same number of stars as circles. Coat both sides of stars with sugar. Place 1 inch apart on ungreased cookie sheets. Bake at 375°F. for 6 to 7 minutes or until slightly puffy but not brown. Remove from cookie sheets; cool completely. To use remaining dough, cut an equal number of stars and circles. Bake as directed above.

In small bowl, combine ¼ cup butter, powdered sugar and vanilla; beat until smooth and fluffy. Add a few drops of whipping cream if necessary for desired spreading consistency. Spoon half of filling into small bowl. Color half of

filling with red food color; color remaining half with green food color. Carefully spread filling to edges of each circle cookie; top with star cookie. Repeat with remaining cookies and filling. **5 to 6 dozen cookies.**

HIGH ALTITUDE—Above 3500 Feet: Increase flour to 2¼ cups. Bake as directed above.

NUTRITION INFORMATION PER SERVING

Serving Size: 1 cookie		Percent U.S. RDA	
Calories	50	Protein	*
Protein	0g	Vitamin A	2%
Carbohydrate	5g	Vitamin C	*
Fat	4g	Thiamine	*
Cholesterol	10mg	Riboflavin	*
Sodium	35mg	Niacin	*
Potassium	5mg	Calcium	*
		Iron	*
		*Contains less than 2%	

Three-Tiered Trees

Three-Tiered Trees

These little stacked trees, made from refrigerator cookies, can be a colorful addition to a holiday cookie plate.

Santa's Stockings

This refrigerator cookie is uniquely shaped to produce a slice-and-bake stocking cookie.

COOKIES

1 cup margarine or butter, softened
1 cup powdered sugar
1 teaspoon vanilla
½ teaspoon green food color
1¾ cups all purpose or unbleached flour
¼ teaspoon salt
¼ cup green colored sugar
72 red cinnamon candies

FROSTING

½ cup powdered sugar
1 to 2 teaspoons milk

In large bowl, beat margarine and 1 cup powdered sugar until light and fluffy. Add vanilla and green food color; blend well. Lightly spoon flour into measuring cup; level off. Add flour and salt; mix well by hand. Divide dough in half. Shape half into 12-inch roll; roll in green colored sugar. Wrap in plastic wrap. Divide remaining half of dough into ⅔ and ⅓ portions. Shape each into 12-inch roll; roll each in green colored sugar. Wrap in plastic wrap; refrigerate rolls about 2 hours.

Heat oven to 375°F. Cut each roll of dough into ⅛-inch slices. Place 1 inch apart on ungreased cookie sheets. Bake at 375°F. for 6 to 8 minutes or until set. Remove from cookie sheets; cool completely.

In small bowl, combine frosting ingredients, adding enough milk for desired spreading consistency; beat until smooth. To make each tree, place a small amount of frosting in center of large circle; top with medium circle.

Place a small amount of frosting in center of medium circle; top with small circle. Attach red cinnamon candy to top of tree with frosting.
6 dozen cookies.

TIP: To make ahead prepare dough, shape into rolls and coat with sugar. Wrap in plastic wrap; freeze. To bake, let dough stand at room temperature to soften slightly. Slice and bake as directed above.

HIGH ALTITUDE—Above 3500 Feet: Increase flour to 2 cups. Bake as directed above.

NUTRITION INFORMATION PER SERVING

Serving Size: 1 cookie		Percent U.S. RDA	
Calories	45	Protein	*
Protein	0g	Vitamin A	2%
Carbohydrate	5g	Vitamin C	*
Fat	3g	Thiamine	*
Cholesterol	0mg	Riboflavin	*
Sodium	40mg	Niacin	*
Potassium	0mg	Calcium	*
		Iron	*
		*Contains less than 2%	

Santa's Stockings

COOKIES

½ cup sugar
½ cup margarine or butter, softened
½ teaspoon vanilla
1 egg
1½ cups all purpose or unbleached flour
¼ teaspoon baking soda
¼ teaspoon salt
10 to 12 drops red or green food color

FROSTING

½ cup powdered sugar
2 teaspoons margarine or butter, softened
2 teaspoons milk

In large bowl, combine sugar, ½ cup margarine, vanilla and egg; beat well. Lightly spoon flour into measuring cup; level off. Stir in flour, baking soda and salt; mix well. Add food color; blend evenly into dough.* Divide dough in half; place each half on sheet of waxed paper. Shape each half into a log 1½ inches in diameter. Wrap in waxed paper; refrigerate ½ hour.

To create stocking shape, carefully mold each log into a slanted "L" shape.** Rewrap; refrigerate until firm, about 3 hours.

Santa's Stockings

Heat oven to 375°F. Cut dough into ⅛-inch slices. (Do not distort stocking shape.) Place 1 inch apart on ungreased cookie sheets. Bake at 375°F. for 5 to 8 minutes or until edges are light golden brown. Immediately remove from cookie sheets; cool completely.

In small bowl, combine all frosting ingredients; beat until smooth. Frost as desired. Let stand until frosting is set. Store in loosely covered container.
5 dozen cookies.

TIPS: *If desired, divide dough in half before adding food color. Color half of dough with red food color; color remaining half of dough with green food color.

**The handle of a wooden spoon works well when shaping the cookie log into the "L" or stocking shape.

HIGH ALTITUDE—Above 3500 Feet: No change.

NUTRITION INFORMATION PER SERVING

Serving Size: 1 cookie		Percent U.S. RDA	
Calories	35	Protein	*
Protein	0g	Vitamin A	*
Carbohydrate	5g	Vitamin C	*
Fat	2g	Thiamine	*
Cholesterol	4mg	Riboflavin	*
Sodium	35mg	Niacin	*
Potassium	5mg	Calcium	*
		Iron	*
		*Contains less than 2%	

Candy Cane Cookies

1¼ cups powdered sugar
1 cup margarine or butter, softened
½ teaspoon vanilla
½ teaspoon peppermint extract
1 egg
2½ cups all purpose or unbleached flour
1 teaspoon baking soda
1 teaspoon cream of tartar
2 tablespoons evaporated milk or half-and-half
Several drops red food color

In large bowl, combine powdered sugar, margarine, vanilla, peppermint extract and egg; beat well. Lightly spoon flour into measuring cup; level off. Stir in flour, baking soda and cream of tartar; mix well. Cover with plastic wrap; refrigerate at least 1 hour for easier handling. In small bowl, combine evaporated milk and food color.

Heat oven to 375°F. On lightly floured surface, roll out ⅓ of dough at a time to ⅛-inch thickness. (Refrigerate remaining dough.) Cut with floured candy-cane-shaped cookie cutter. Place 1 inch apart on ungreased cookie sheets. Using small paintbrush and evaporated milk mixture, paint stripes on cookies. Bake at 375°F. for 5 to 7 minutes or until edges are light golden brown. Immediately remove from cookie sheets; cool completely. Store in loosely covered container.
4 dozen cookies.

HIGH ALTITUDE — Above 3500 Feet: Decrease baking soda to ½ teaspoon. Bake at 375°F. for 5 to 7 minutes.

NUTRITION INFORMATION PER SERVING
Serving Size: 1 cookie		Percent U.S. RDA	
Calories	70	Protein	*
Protein	1g	Vitamin A	2%
Carbohydrate	8g	Vitamin C	*
Fat	4g	Thiamine	2%
Cholesterol	4mg	Riboflavin	2%
Sodium	70mg	Niacin	*
Potassium	10mg	Calcium	*
		Iron	*
*Contains less than 2%			

White Chocolate Almond Bars

2 ounces (2 squares) premier white baking bar, chopped
½ cup margarine or butter
¾ cup sugar
2 eggs
1 teaspoon almond extract
⅔ cup all purpose or unbleached flour
½ teaspoon baking powder
¼ teaspoon salt
½ cup chopped almonds
1 tablespoon powdered sugar

Heat oven to 350°F. Grease and lightly flour bottom only of 8- or 9-inch square pan. Melt chocolate in medium saucepan over very low heat, stirring constantly until smooth. Add margarine; whisk until melted.* Remove from heat; stir in sugar. Whisk in eggs 1 at a time. Add almond extract. Lightly spoon flour into measuring cup; level off. Add flour, baking powder, salt and almonds to chocolate mixture; mix well. Spread in greased and floured pan. Bake at 350°F. for 25 to 35 minutes or until golden brown and center is set. Cool completely. Sprinkle with powdered sugar; cut into bars.
24 bars.

TIP: *Premier white baking bar melts slower than regular chocolate. A wire whisk works well when blending the chocolate and margarine.

HIGH ALTITUDE — Above 3500 Feet: Decrease sugar to ⅔ cup and increase flour to ¾ cup. Bake as directed above.

NUTRITION INFORMATION PER SERVING
Serving Size: 1 bar		Percent U.S. RDA	
Calories	110	Protein	2%
Protein	2g	Vitamin A	2%
Carbohydrate	11g	Vitamin C	*
Fat	6g	Thiamine	2%
Cholesterol	18mg	Riboflavin	4%
Sodium	80mg	Niacin	*
Potassium	40mg	Calcium	2%
		Iron	*
*Contains less than 2%			

O Christmas Tree Cookies

O Christmas Tree Cookies

¾ cup sugar
¾ cup margarine or butter, softened
1 (3-ounce) package cream cheese, softened
¼ teaspoon peppermint extract
1 egg yolk
2¼ cups all purpose or unbleached flour
½ teaspoon salt
 Colored sugars
 Frosting tinted as desired
 Edible glitter*
 Assorted small candies

In large bowl, beat sugar, margarine and cream cheese until light and fluffy. Add peppermint extract and egg yolk; blend well. Lightly spoon flour into measuring cup; level off. Stir in flour and salt; mix well. Cover with plastic wrap; refrigerate 2 hours for easier handling.

Heat oven to 375°F. On well-floured surface, roll out dough ⅓ at a time to ⅛-inch thickness. (Refrigerate remaining dough.) Cut with assorted sizes and shapes of tree cookie cutters. Place 1 inch apart on ungreased cookie sheets. Colored sugar can be sprinkled on cookies before baking. Bake at 375°F. for 5 to 8 minutes or until edges are light golden brown. Cool 1 minute; remove from cookie sheets. Cool completely.

Frost cookies and decorate with edible glitter and/or candies as desired. Let stand until frosting is set. Store between sheets of waxed paper in loosely covered container.

About 4 dozen cookies.

TIP: *Edible glitter is available at kitchen specialty shops.

HIGH ALTITUDE — Above 3500 Feet: No change.

NUTRITION INFORMATION PER SERVING

Serving Size: 1 cookie		Percent U.S. RDA	
Calories	80	Protein	*
Protein	1g	Vitamin A	2%
Carbohydrate	10g	Vitamin C	*
Fat	4g	Thiamine	2%
Cholesterol	6mg	Riboflavin	2%
Sodium	60mg	Niacin	*
Potassium	10mg	Calcium	*
		Iron	*
		*Contains less than 2%	

O Christmas Tree Cookies

Edible glitter comes in a festive array of colors and is available at kitchen specialty shops. It's a dazzling garnish for holiday treats.

Springerle

Springerle

Springerle

These German "picture cookies" must dry overnight before being baked. The dough is pressed into special molds, or designs are rolled on with a special springerle rolling pin. The cookies contain anise oil, which gives them their distinctive licorice flavor. Storing the baked cookies for several weeks helps develop this flavor.

4 eggs
2 cups sugar
4 to 6 drops anise oil or ½ to 1 teaspoon anise extract
3½ cups all purpose or unbleached flour
1 teaspoon baking powder
¼ teaspoon salt

In large bowl, beat eggs on high speed until very thick, about 3 to 4 minutes. Gradually beat in sugar; continue beating for 15 minutes. Beat in anise oil. Lightly spoon flour into measuring cup; level off. Stir in remaining ingredients. Cover with plastic wrap; refrigerate 1 hour for easier handling.

Lightly grease cookie sheets. On well-floured surface, roll out dough into ½-inch-thick rectangular shape the same width as springerle rolling pin.* Roll designs into dough. Cut cookies along design lines and place on greased cookie sheets. Cover with cloth; let stand in cool place overnight.

Heat oven to 375°F. Uncover cookies and place in oven; immediately reduce oven temperature to 300°F. Bake 20 to 25 minutes or until set. Immediately remove from cookie sheets; cool completely. Store in tightly covered container several weeks before serving.
4 dozen cookies.

TIP: *If springerle mold is used, roll out dough ½ inch thick and press floured mold into dough; lift off and cut along design lines.

HIGH ALTITUDE — Above 3500 Feet: No change.

NUTRITION INFORMATION PER SERVING

Serving Size: 1 cookie		Percent U.S. RDA	
Calories	70	Protein	2%
Protein	1g	Vitamin A	*
Carbohydrate	15g	Vitamin C	*
Fat	1g	Thiamine	4%
Cholesterol	18mg	Riboflavin	4%
Sodium	20mg	Niacin	2%
Potassium	15mg	Calcium	*
		Iron	2%
		*Contains less than 2%	

Date-Filled Meringues

1 cup dates, ground*
½ cup walnuts, ground*
½ teaspoon vanilla
2 egg whites
⅔ cup sugar
½ teaspoon vanilla
Food color, if desired

Heat oven to 250°F. Generously grease cookie sheets. In medium bowl, combine dates, walnuts and ½ teaspoon vanilla; mix well. Shape ½ teaspoonfuls of mixture into balls; place on sheet of waxed paper.

In small bowl, beat egg whites until soft peaks form. Gradually add sugar, beating until stiff peaks form. Stir in ½ teaspoon vanilla and food color. Drop balls 1 at a time into meringue. Using spoon, coat well to form 1-inch balls. Place on greased cookie sheets; swirl top of meringue with spoon. Bake at 250°F. for 30 minutes. Immediately remove from cookie sheets; cool completely.
4 dozen cookies.

TIP: *Dates and walnuts can be ground in food processor or food mill.

NUTRITION INFORMATION PER SERVING

Serving Size: 1 cookie		Percent U.S. RDA	
Calories	30	Protein	*
Protein	0g	Vitamin A	*
Carbohydrate	6g	Vitamin C	*
Fat	1g	Thiamine	*
Cholesterol	0mg	Riboflavin	*
Sodium	0mg	Niacin	*
Potassium	30mg	Calcium	*
		Iron	*
		*Contains less than 2%	

Apricot-Raisin Bars

BASE
1½ cups all-purpose or unbleached flour
1¾ cups quick-cooking rolled oats
1 cup firmly packed brown sugar
1 cup margarine or butter

FILLING
1 (12-ounce) jar apricot preserves
½ cup chopped almonds
½ cup raisins
½ teaspoon almond extract

Heat oven to 350°F. Lightly spoon flour into measuring cup; level off. In large bowl, combine flour, oats and brown sugar. Using fork or pastry blender, cut margarine into flour mixture until mixture resembles coarse crumbs. Press 3 cups of base mixture in ungreased 13 × 9-inch pan.

In small bowl, combine all filling ingredients; blend well. Spoon filling evenly over base. Sprinkle remaining crumb mixture over filling. Bake at 350°F. for 25 to 35 minutes or until golden brown. Cool completely; cut into bars.
36 bars.

HIGH ALTITUDE — Above 3500 Feet: No change.

NUTRITION INFORMATION PER SERVING

Serving Size: 1 bar		Percent U.S. RDA	
Calories	140	Protein	2%
Protein	2g	Vitamin A	4%
Carbohydrate	21g	Vitamin C	*
Fat	6g	Thiamine	4%
Cholesterol	0mg	Riboflavin	2%
Sodium	65mg	Niacin	2%
Potassium	80mg	Calcium	*
		Iron	4%
		*Contains less than 2%	

Date-Filled Meringues

The egg white, unlike the yolk, is free of fat and cholesterol and contains only 16 calories. When beaten, it inflates to eight times its original volume, accounting for the wonderful lightness of meringues.

Apricot-Raisin Bars

An easy-to-make bar that is sure to please apricot fans.

Jingle Bells

What a fast and easy way to make holiday cookies! These bell-shaped cookies are made in two different colors for an attractive addition to a holiday cookie tray.

COOK'S NOTE

Bars

For a better appearance and to reduce crumbling, cool bar cookies in the pan before cutting unless otherwise instructed. Bar cookies may be stored, tightly covered, in the baking pan. For food safety, some frostings, fillings or other ingredients may require refrigerator storage as stated in the recipe.

Jingle Bells

1 (20-ounce) package refrigerated sliceable sugar cookie dough
1 tablespoon green colored sugar
1 tablespoon red colored sugar
17 green candy-coated chocolate pieces
17 red candy-coated chocolate pieces

Heat oven to 350°F. Cut roll of dough in half crosswise, forming 2 rolls. Coat sides of 1 roll with green sugar; coat other roll with red sugar. Refrigerate rolls until ready to slice. To bake, cut dough into ⅛ to ¼-inch slices. Place 2 inches apart on ungreased cookie sheets. To form bell, fold in sides of slices as shown in diagram; place candy piece on bell for clapper.

Bake at 350°F. for 8 to 12 minutes or until edges are light golden brown. Cool 2 minutes; remove from cookie sheets. Cool completely.
34 cookies.

NUTRITION INFORMATION PER SERVING

Serving Size: 1 cookie		Percent U.S. RDA	
Calories	80	Protein	*
Protein	1g	Vitamin A	*
Carbohydrate	11g	Vitamin C	*
Fat	3g	Thiamine	*
Cholesterol	2mg	Riboflavin	*
Sodium	70mg	Niacin	*
Potassium	10mg	Calcium	*
		Iron	*
		*Contains less than 2%	

[Diagram for Jingle Bells]

Diagram for Jingle Bells

Cranberry-Date Bars

1 (16-ounce) can whole berry cranberry sauce
1 cup chopped dates
1¼ cups all purpose or unbleached flour
1 cup quick-cooking rolled oats
⅔ cup firmly packed brown sugar
½ teaspoon cinnamon
½ cup margarine or butter, softened

Heat oven to 350°F. Grease 9-inch square pan. In medium saucepan, combine cranberry sauce and dates. Bring to a boil; reduce heat and simmer 5 minutes, stirring frequently. Cool slightly.

Lightly spoon flour into measuring cup; level off. In medium bowl, combine flour, oats, brown sugar and cinnamon; mix well. Using fork or pastry blender, cut margarine into flour mixture until mixture resembles coarse crumbs. Press half of mixture firmly in bottom of greased pan. Spread evenly with cranberry-date mixture. Sprinkle with remaining crumb mixture; pat lightly. Bake at 350°F. for 30 to 35 minutes or until golden brown. Cool completely; cut into bars.
24 bars.

HIGH ALTITUDE—Above 3500 Feet: No change.

NUTRITION INFORMATION PER SERVING

Serving Size: 1 bar		Percent U.S. RDA	
Calories	140	Protein	2%
Protein	1g	Vitamin A	2%
Carbohydrate	26g	Vitamin C	*
Fat	4g	Thiamine	6%
Cholesterol	0mg	Riboflavin	2%
Sodium	50mg	Niacin	2%
Potassium	95mg	Calcium	*
		Iron	4%
		*Contains less than 2%	

Pictured Clockwise from left: Cranberry-Date Bars; Cranberry Cheesecake Bars; Jingle Bells

Cranberry Cheesecake Bars

CRUST
- 1 package pudding-included butter recipe cake mix
- ½ cup margarine or butter, softened
- 1 egg
- ¼ cup chopped pecans

FILLING
- 1 (8-ounce) package cream cheese, softened
- ¼ cup powdered sugar
- ½ teaspoon vanilla
- 1 egg
- 1 (16-ounce) can whole berry cranberry sauce
- ¼ teaspoon nutmeg

Heat oven to 350°F. In large bowl, combine cake mix, margarine and 1 egg at low speed until crumbly. Add pecans; mix well. Press evenly in bottom of ungreased 13 × 9-inch pan. Bake at 350°F. for 5 to 8 minutes or until crust is set. (Crust will not be browned.)

In small bowl, combine cream cheese, powdered sugar, vanilla and 1 egg; beat until smooth. In another small bowl, combine cranberry sauce and nutmeg; blend well. Carefully pour cream cheese mixture over partially baked crust. Spoon cranberry sauce lengthwise in 3 rows over cream cheese. Pull knife through cranberry sauce and cream cheese mixture to form swirls. Bake at 350°F. for 30 to 40 minutes or until cream cheese mixture is set. Cool completely; cut into bars.

36 bars.

HIGH ALTITUDE—Above 3500 Feet: No change.

Cranberry Cheesecake Bars

A crumb crust made from cake mix makes this bar very easy. Swirls of cranberries and cream cheese top it off just perfectly.

NUTRITION INFORMATION PER SERVING

Serving Size: 1 bar		Percent U.S. RDA	
Calories	130	Protein	2%
Protein	2g	Vitamin A	4%
Carbohydrate	18g	Vitamin C	*
Fat	7g	Thiamine	2%
Cholesterol	19mg	Riboflavin	2%
Sodium	150mg	Niacin	*
Potassium	25mg	Calcium	2%
		Iron	*

*Contains less than 2%

# A Seasonful of Sweets

Create Your Own Sugarplum Visions

Christmas is a season of memory-making with family, with friends. This selection of sweets will help create—or rekindle—those Christmas memories. From brickles to barks, toffees to truffles, crunches to clusters, these candies and confections offer an enticing addition to your holiday celebrations. Give them as gifts to co-workers. Present them as a thank-you to a host or hostess. Send them to faraway family members as a reminder of holidays at home. Surprise a shut-in with an assortment. Or serve them as the finishing touch to a festive meal.

But if nightmares of candy thermometers dance through your head, take heart. Only two recipes—Taffy and Chocolate Swirl Almond Toffee—require a candy thermometer. Some, like Candied Pecans and Brickle Bark, have only three ingredients. And many, including Microwave Chunky Peanut Butter Cups and Easy Chocolate Truffles, can be made in the microwave or, like Apricot-Raisin Brandy Balls, require no cooking at all!

Since many of these sweets are so simple to make, why not gather a group of friends for a candy exchange? Each person can bring a preassigned candy, or the group can meet at someone's home to prepare them together. Then everyone gets a unique and tasty assortment to sample.

Besides sampling them, part of the fun of candies is giving them. They lend themselves to beautiful gift wraps and masses of curled ribbon, sparkly tissues and glittery boxes. Just imagine a dozen Long-stemmed Cherries Supreme presented in a cloud of pink tissue and tied up with silver ribbon. For the chocolate lover on your list, pack a melt-in-your-mouth assortment of fudges in pretty tins. You can create eight different fudge varieties from just two easy recipes: Chocolate Fudge and Vanilla Fudge. Who says gifts need to be expensive to be enjoyed!

Brickle Bark

10 ounces vanilla-flavored candy
  coating, cut into pieces
1 (6-ounce) package almond
  brickle baking chips
10 ounces chocolate-flavored candy
  coating, cut into pieces

MICROWAVE DIRECTIONS: Line 2 cookie sheets with waxed paper. In 1-quart microwave-safe bowl or 4-cup microwave-safe measuring cup, melt vanilla coating on MEDIUM for 2½ to 3 minutes or until melted, stirring once halfway through heating. Stir until smooth. Stir in half of brickle chips. Spread mixture on waxed paper-lined cookie sheet. Repeat using chocolate coating and remaining brickle chips. Refrigerate until set. Break into pieces. Store in airtight container in cool, dry place.
1 pound 10 ounces.

CONVENTIONAL DIRECTIONS: Line 2 cookie sheets with waxed paper. In 2 medium saucepans over low heat, melt vanilla coating and chocolate coating separately, stirring constantly. Continue as directed above.

NUTRITION INFORMATION PER SERVING

Serving Size: 1 ounce		Percent U.S. RDA	
Calories	150	Protein	2%
Protein	1g	Vitamin A	*
Carbohydrate	17g	Vitamin C	*
Fat	9g	Thiamine	*
Cholesterol	5mg	Riboflavin	2%
Sodium	20mg	Niacin	*
Potassium	65mg	Calcium	4%
		Iron	*

*Contains less than 2%

Christmas Bark

16 ounces vanilla-flavored candy
  coating, cut into pieces
1 cup pecan halves
¾ cup red candied cherries, halved
¾ cup green candied cherries,
  halved

Line cookie sheet with waxed paper. Melt candy coating in medium saucepan over low heat, stirring constantly. Add remaining ingredients; toss to coat. Spread mixture on waxed paper-lined cookie sheet. Let stand until set. Break into pieces. **18 ounces.**

MICROWAVE DIRECTIONS: Line cookie sheet with waxed paper. Place candy coating in 2-quart microwave-safe bowl or 8-cup microwave-safe measuring cup. Microwave on MEDIUM for 3 to 4½ minutes, stirring once halfway through melting. Stir until smooth. Continue as directed above.

NUTRITION INFORMATION PER SERVING

Serving Size: 1 ounce		Percent U.S. RDA	
Calories	220	Protein	2%
Protein	2g	Vitamin A	*
Carbohydrate	28g	Vitamin C	*
Fat	12g	Thiamine	2%
Cholesterol	6mg	Riboflavin	4%
Sodium	25mg	Niacin	*
Potassium	100mg	Calcium	4%
		Iron	*

*Contains less than 2%

Pictured on preceding pages clockwise from upper left: Caramel Corn, page 31; Raspberry Divinity Squares, page 36; Peppermint Jelly Candy, page 35; Easy Chocolate Truffles, page 39; Candied Pecans, page 43

Pictured left to right: Christmas Bark; Chocolate Swirl Almond Toffee

Chocolate Swirl Almond Toffee

TOFFEE
 1 cup butter or margarine
 2 tablespoons light corn syrup
 2 tablespoons water
 1 cup sugar
 1 cup chopped almonds

TOPPING
 ½ cup semi-sweet chocolate chips
 ½ cup vanilla milk chips*

Line 15 × 10 × 1-inch baking pan with foil; butter foil. In heavy 2-quart saucepan, combine butter, corn syrup, water and sugar. Cook over medium heat until sugar dissolves and mixture boils, stirring constantly. Using candy thermometer, continue cooking to 290°F. (soft-crack stage), stirring occasionally. Remove from heat. Quickly stir in almonds. Pour mixture into buttered, foil-lined pan. Let stand 2 to 3 minutes to harden.

In small bowl, combine chocolate and vanilla milk chips. Sprinkle chips over hot toffee; let stand 1 to 1½ minutes to soften. With knife, swirl softened chips over toffee. Refrigerate until chocolate is set. Break into pieces.
25 ounces.

TIP: *Three ounces vanilla-flavored candy coating can be substituted for vanilla milk chips; chop into ¼-inch pieces.

NUTRITION INFORMATION PER SERVING

Serving Size: 1 ounce		Percent U.S. RDA	
Calories	170	Protein	2%
Protein	1g	Vitamin A	6%
Carbohydrate	14g	Vitamin C	*
Fat	12g	Thiamine	*
Cholesterol	1mg	Riboflavin	2%
Sodium	90mg	Niacin	*
Potassium	65mg	Calcium	2%
		Iron	*
		*Contains less than 2%	

Chocolate Swirl Almond Toffee

This buttery, crunchy candy is topped with decadent swirls of white and dark chocolate.

Microwave Cashew Crunch; Brickle Bark, page 28

Microwave Cashew Crunch

1 cup sugar
½ cup light corn syrup
1 cup cashews or peanuts
1 teaspoon butter or margarine
1 teaspoon vanilla
1 teaspoon baking soda

MICROWAVE DIRECTIONS: Line cookie sheet with foil; lightly butter foil. In 8-cup microwave-safe measuring cup or medium microwave-safe bowl, combine sugar and corn syrup. Microwave on HIGH for 4 minutes; stir. Add cashews; blend well. Microwave on HIGH for 3½ to 4½ minutes or until mixture is light brown; stir in butter and vanilla. Microwave on HIGH for 1 minute. Add baking soda; stir quickly to blend. Pour immediately onto buttered, foil-lined cookie sheet, spreading mixture quickly with wooden spoon. Cool 30 minutes; break into pieces. Store in airtight container. **15 ounces.**

NUTRITION INFORMATION PER SERVING

Serving Size: 1 ounce		Percent U.S. RDA	
Calories	140	Protein	2%
Protein	1g	Vitamin A	*
Carbohydrate	25g	Vitamin C	*
Fat	5g	Thiamine	*
Cholesterol	1mg	Riboflavin	*
Sodium	85mg	Niacin	*
Potassium	55mg	Calcium	*
		Iron	6%
		*Contains less than 2%	

Caramel Corn

6 cups popped popcorn
½ cup toasted slivered almonds, if
    desired*
¾ cup firmly packed brown sugar
½ cup margarine or butter
2 tablespoons light corn syrup
⅛ teaspoon salt
¼ teaspoon baking soda

MICROWAVE DIRECTIONS: Combine popcorn and almonds in a large microwave-safe bowl. In 4-cup microwave-safe measuring cup, combine brown sugar, margarine, corn syrup and salt. Microwave on HIGH for 2 minutes; stir. Microwave on HIGH for 2 to 3 minutes or until mixture comes to a rolling boil. Stir in baking soda; mix well. Pour over popcorn and almonds; toss until coated. Microwave on HIGH for 2 minutes. Immediately spread on foil or waxed paper to cool. **6 cups.**

CONVENTIONAL DIRECTIONS: Heat oven to 250°F. Spread popcorn in 15 × 10 × 1-inch baking pan; sprinkle almonds over popcorn. In large saucepan, combine brown sugar, margarine, *2 tablespoons water*, corn syrup and salt; bring to a boil over medium heat. Boil 2 minutes, stirring constantly. Remove from heat. Stir in baking soda; mix well. Pour over popcorn and almonds; toss until coated. Bake at 250°F. for 15 minutes; stir. Continue baking for an additional 15 minutes; stir. Bake an additional 5 minutes. Immediately spread on foil or waxed paper to cool.

TIP: *To toast almonds, spread in thin layer in microwave-safe pie pan. Microwave on HIGH for 5 to 7 minutes or until light golden brown, stirring frequently. Or spread almonds on cookie sheet; bake at 350°F. for 5 to 10 minutes or until light golden brown, stirring occasionally.

NUTRITION INFORMATION PER SERVING

Serving Size: 1 cup		Percent U.S. RDA	
Calories	360	Protein	6%
Protein	4g	Vitamin A	10%
Carbohydrate	45g	Vitamin C	*
Fat	20g	Thiamine	4%
Cholesterol	0mg	Riboflavin	4%
Sodium	280mg	Niacin	2%
Potassium	200mg	Calcium	4%
		Iron	10%
*Contains less than 2%			

Caramel Nut Candy Bars

8 ounces (about 30) caramels
3 tablespoons milk
3 tablespoons margarine or butter
1 cup powdered sugar
1 (12-ounce) can (2½ cups)
    peanuts

Lightly grease 8-inch square pan. In top of double boiler, combine caramels and milk. Cook over hot water until caramels are melted, stirring occasionally. Remove from heat. Add margarine; mix well. Stir in powdered sugar; beat by hand until smooth. Stir in peanuts. With buttered fingers, press mixture in greased pan. Refrigerate 1 to 2 hours or until firm; cut into bars. Store in refrigerator. **18 bars.**

MICROWAVE DIRECTIONS: Lightly grease 8-inch square pan. In medium microwave-safe bowl, combine caramels and *1 tablespoon milk*. Microwave on MEDIUM for 5 to 7 minutes or until caramels are melted, stirring every 2 minutes. Continue as directed above.

NUTRITION INFORMATION PER SERVING

Serving Size: 1 bar		Percent U.S. RDA	
Calories	200	Protein	8%
Protein	5g	Vitamin A	*
Carbohydrate	19g	Vitamin C	*
Fat	13g	Thiamine	6%
Cholesterol	0mg	Riboflavin	2%
Sodium	210mg	Niacin	10%
Potassium	150mg	Calcium	2%
		Iron	2%
*Contains less than 2%			

Caramel Corn

Microwave preparation and excellent flavor make this recipe a must for holiday snacking.

Caramel Nut Candy Bars

You may want to enlist little helpers to unwrap the caramels for these sumptuous bars.

Chocolate Fudge

Chocolate Fudge

This easy version of a popular holiday candy is just as flavorful and satiny as the old-fashioned version. Note all of the varieties you can make from this one simple recipe.

> 🎄
> ## COOK'S NOTE
>
> ### Making Candy in the Microwave
>
> When making candy in the microwave, avoid boil-overs by using a container that holds two to three times more than the volume being cooked. Do not cover the container. An uncovered container allows unwanted moisture to escape and simplifies stirring.

2½ cups sugar
½ cup margarine or butter
1 (5-ounce) can (⅔ cup) evaporated milk
1 (7-ounce) jar (2 cups) marshmallow creme
1 (12-ounce) package (2 cups) semi-sweet chocolate chips
¾ cup chopped walnuts
1 teaspoon vanilla

Line 9-inch square or 13 × 9-inch pan with foil so that foil extends over sides of pan; butter foil. In large saucepan, combine sugar, margarine and evaporated milk. Bring to a boil over medium heat, stirring constantly. Boil 5 minutes, stirring constantly. Remove from heat. Add marshmallow creme and chocolate chips; blend until smooth. Stir in walnuts and vanilla. Pour into buttered, foil-lined pan. Cool to room temperature. Score fudge into 36 or 48 squares. Refrigerate until firm.

Remove fudge from pan by lifting foil; remove foil from sides of fudge. Using large knife, cut through scored lines. Store in refrigerator.
About 3 pounds (36 or 48 squares).

MICROWAVE DIRECTIONS: Line 9-inch square or 13 × 9-inch pan with foil so that foil extends over sides of pan; butter foil. In 2-quart microwave-safe bowl, combine sugar, margarine and evaporated milk. Microwave on HIGH for 6 to 8 minutes or until mixture comes to a rolling boil, stirring twice during cooking. Add marshmallow creme and chocolate chips; blend until smooth. Stir in walnuts and vanilla. Continue as directed above.

VARIATIONS:

BUTTERSCOTCH FUDGE: Prepare fudge as directed above, substituting 1 (12-ounce) package butterscotch chips for chocolate chips and pecans for walnuts.

CONFETTI FUDGE: Prepare fudge as directed above, substituting 2 cups candy-coated chocolate pieces for walnuts. Stir 1½ cups of the chocolate pieces into fudge with vanilla. Pour into buttered, foil-lined pan. Sprinkle remaining ½ cup chocolate pieces over top; press lightly into warm fudge. Cool to room temperature. Do not refrigerate before cutting. Store in refrigerator; let stand at room temperature before serving.

TURTLE FUDGE: Prepare fudge as directed above, substituting cashews for walnuts and adding 24 quartered caramels with cashews and vanilla. Cool to room temperature. Do not refrigerate before cutting. Store in refrigerator; let stand at room temperature before serving.

NUTRITION INFORMATION PER SERVING

Serving Size: 1 ounce Chocolate Fudge		Percent U.S. RDA	
Calories	120	Protein	*
Protein	1g	Vitamin A	*
Carbohydrate	18g	Vitamin C	*
Fat	6g	Thiamine	*
Cholesterol	0mg	Riboflavin	*
Sodium	30mg	Niacin	*
Potassium	45mg	Calcium	*
		Iron	*

*Contains less than 2%

Pictured top to bottom: Turtle Fudge; Peppermint Candy Fudge, page 34; Christmas Fudge, page 34; Confetti Fudge

Vanilla Fudge

2½ cups sugar
½ cup margarine or butter
1 (5-ounce) can (⅔ cup) evaporated milk
1 (7-ounce) jar (2 cups) marshmallow creme
8 ounces vanilla-flavored candy coating, cut into pieces
¾ cup chopped walnuts
1 teaspoon vanilla

Line 9-inch square or 13 × 9-inch pan with foil so that foil extends over sides of pan; butter foil. In large saucepan, combine sugar, margarine and evaporated milk. Bring to a boil over medium heat, stirring constantly. Boil 5 minutes, stirring constantly. Remove from heat. Add marshmallow creme and vanilla coating; blend until smooth. Stir in walnuts and vanilla. Pour into buttered, foil-lined pan. Cool to room temperature. Score fudge into 36 or 48 squares. Refrigerate until firm.

Remove fudge from pan by lifting foil; remove foil from sides of fudge. Using large knife, cut through scored lines. Store in refrigerator.

About 2½ pounds (36 to 48 squares).

MICROWAVE DIRECTIONS: Not recommended.

VARIATIONS:

CHRISTMAS FUDGE: Prepare fudge as directed above, substituting ½ cup chopped almonds for walnuts and ¼ teaspoon almond extract for vanilla. Stir in ½ cup chopped dates and ½ cup chopped red candied cherries with almonds and almond extract.

EGGNOG FUDGE: Prepare fudge as directed above, substituting ⅔ cup eggnog for evaporated milk and ½ to 1 teaspoon rum extract for vanilla.

PEANUT BUTTER FUDGE: Prepare fudge as directed above, using 6 ounces vanilla coating. Add ½ cup peanut butter with marshmallow creme and vanilla coating. Substitute ¾ cup chopped dry roasted peanuts for walnuts.

PEPPERMINT CANDY FUDGE: Prepare fudge as directed above, substituting ½ cup finely crushed peppermint candy for walnuts. Omit vanilla. Add desired amount of red food color with crushed candies.

PISTACHIO FUDGE: Prepare fudge as directed above, substituting pistachios for walnuts. Add desired amount of green food color with pistachios.

NUTRITION INFORMATION PER SERVING

Serving Size: 1 ounce Vanilla Fudge		Percent U.S. RDA	
Calories	130	Protein	*
Protein	1g	Vitamin A	2%
Carbohydrate	21g	Vitamin C	*
Fat	5g	Thiamine	*
Cholesterol	1mg	Riboflavin	*
Sodium	40mg	Niacin	*
Potassium	45mg	Calcium	2%
		Iron	*
		*Contains less than 2%	

COOK'S NOTE

White Chocolate

White chocolate, according to the Food and Drug Administration, is really not chocolate at all because it does not contain "chocolate liquor" from the cocoa bean. It is a blend of cocoa butter, sugar, milk and flavorings and is available in different forms:

• Imported varieties in bar form
• Vanilla-flavored candy coating or compound chocolate
• Vanilla-milk flavored chips

The imported European varieties are made with cocoa butter. Candy coating, compound chocolate and chips are made with coconut, soybean or palm kernel oil.

White chocolate has a milk flavor similar to milk chocolate. It can be found in specialty food shops, candy stores and the baking section of some supermarkets.

Microwave Meltaway Fudge

1 (14-ounce) can sweetened condensed milk (not evaporated)
1 (12-ounce) package (2 cups) semi-sweet chocolate chips
1 teaspoon vanilla

MICROWAVE DIRECTIONS: Line 8-inch square pan with foil so foil extends over sides of pan; butter foil. in 2½-quart microwave-safe bowl or 8-cup microwave-safe measuring cup, combine condensed milk and chocolate chips. Microwave on HIGH for 1½ to 1¾ minutes or until melted, stirring once during cooking. Stir until smooth. Add vanilla; stir well. Pour into buttered, foil-lined pan. Refrigerate until set.

Remove fudge from pan by lifting foil; remove foil from sides of fudge. Using large knife, cut fudge into squares. Store in airtight container in refrigerator. **1 pound 9 ounces.**

CONVENTIONAL DIRECTIONS: Line 8-inch square pan with foil so foil extends over sides of pan; butter foil. In medium saucepan over low heat, combine condensed milk and chocolate chips; cook until chips are melted and mixture is smooth, stirring constantly. Continue as directed above.

VARIATIONS:

BLACK FOREST FUDGE: Prepare fudge as directed above, substituting ¼ teaspoon almond extract for vanilla. Stir ⅔ cup chopped red candied cherries, ½ cup chopped almonds and ½ cup miniature marshmallows into melted chocolate mixture. Continue as directed above.

ROCKY ROAD FUDGE: Prepare fudge as directed above, adding 1 cup miniature marshmallows and ½ cup chopped nuts to melted chocolate mixture with vanilla.

NUTRITION INFORMATION PER SERVING

Serving Size: 1 ounce Chocolate Fudge		Percent U.S. RDA	
Calories	140	Protein	2%
Protein	2g	Vitamin A	*
Carbohydrate	19g	Vitamin C	*
Fat	7g	Thiamine	*
Cholesterol	7mg	Riboflavin	6%
Sodium	25mg	Niacin	*
Potassium	125mg	Calcium	6%
		Iron	2%
		*Contains less than 2%	

Peppermint Jelly Candy

2 tablespoons water
2 (3-ounce) packages liquid fruit pectin
½ teaspoon baking soda
1 cup sugar
1 cup light corn syrup
½ teaspoon peppermint extract
3 drops green food color
Sugar or coarse sugar

Line 8-inch square pan with foil; butter foil. In small saucepan, combine water and pectin. Stir in baking soda. In medium saucepan, combine 1 cup sugar and corn syrup. Cook both mixtures over high heat until foam starts to disappear on pectin mixture and sugar mixture comes to *full rolling boil* (one that cannot be stirred down), about 3 to 5 minutes, stirring both constantly. Slowly pour pectin mixture into sugar mixture, stirring constantly. Continue to boil for 2 minutes, stirring constantly. Remove from heat; stir in peppermint extract and food color. Pour into foil-lined pan. Cool until firm.

Remove candy from pan by lifting foil. With wet knife or scissors, cut into small pieces or desired shapes. Roll in sugar. Store loosely covered. **64 candies.**

NUTRITION INFORMATION PER SERVING

Serving Size: 1 candy		Percent U.S. RDA	
Calories	30	Protein	*
Protein	0g	Vitamin A	*
Carbohydrate	7g	Vitamin C	*
Fat	0g	Thiamine	*
Cholesterol	0mg	Riboflavin	*
Sodium	10mg	Niacin	*
Potassium	5mg	Calcium	*
		Iron	*
		*Contains less than 2%	

Microwave Meltaway Fudge

Create a flavorful assortment of fudges from this one easy recipe.

Peppermint Jelly Candy

For best results, follow the directions carefully to avoid undercooking the mixtures. No candy thermometer is necessary for this old-fashioned candy shop candy.

Raspberry Divinity Squares

Raspberry Divinity Squares

Update this old-fashioned candy by cooking the syrup in the microwave. The candy mixture is spread in a pan and cut into squares.

3 cups sugar
¾ cup light corn syrup
¾ cup water
3 egg whites
1 (3-ounce) package raspberry-flavor gelatin
⅔ cup chopped blanched almonds
½ teaspoon almond extract

MICROWAVE DIRECTIONS: (An electric stand mixer is required for this candy since a portable hand mixer might not be powerful enough to beat the thick mixture.) Line 12 × 8-inch (2-quart) baking dish with foil so that foil extends over sides of dish; butter foil. In 2-quart microwave-safe measuring cup, combine sugar, corn syrup and water. Microwave on HIGH for 17 to 18 minutes or until microwave candy thermometer reaches 260°F. (hard-ball stage), stirring twice during cooking.

Meanwhile, in large bowl beat egg whites until soft peaks form. Gradually add gelatin, beating until egg whites are stiff and glossy. Pour syrup mixture in steady *thin* stream over egg whites, beating at high speed until mixture holds its shape, about 3 to 6 minutes. Stir in almonds and almond extract. Spread evenly in buttered, foil-lined dish. Let stand at room temperature until completely cool and set, about 4 hours or overnight. Cut into 1-inch squares. (Dip knife into hot water if necessary to minimize sticking.) Store in airtight container in cool, dry place.
2 pounds.

NUTRITION INFORMATION PER SERVING

Serving Size: 1 ounce		Percent U.S. RDA	
Calories	120	Protein	*
Protein	1g	Vitamin A	*
Carbohydrate	27g	Vitamin C	*
Fat	1g	Thiamine	*
Cholesterol	0mg	Riboflavin	2%
Sodium	20mg	Niacin	*
Potassium	30mg	Calcium	*
		Iron	2%
*Contains less than 2%			

Fruit and Nut Clusters

Fruit and Nut Clusters

To add color contrast to your candy tray, prepare one recipe using the chocolate chips and another using the vanilla milk chips.

1 (12-ounce) package (2 cups) semi-sweet chocolate or vanilla milk chips
½ cup toasted slivered almonds*
½ cup chopped dates
½ cup chopped red candied cherries
8 red candied cherries, quartered, if desired

Line cookie sheets with waxed paper. Melt chips in medium saucepan over low heat; stir until smooth. Stir in almonds, dates and chopped cherries. Drop by teaspoonfuls onto waxed paper-lined cookie sheets. Garnish each with candied cherry piece. Refrigerate until set. Store in airtight container in cool, dry place.
32 candies.

MICROWAVE DIRECTIONS: Line cookie sheets with waxed paper. In medium microwave-safe bowl, microwave chips on MEDIUM for 3 to 4 minutes, stirring once halfway through cooking. Stir until smooth. Continue as directed above.

TIP: *To toast almonds, spread on cookie sheet; bake at 375°F. for 5 to 10 minutes or until light golden brown. Or, spread in thin layer in microwave-safe pie pan. Microwave on HIGH for 3 to 40 minutes or until light golden brown, stirring frequently.

NUTRITION INFORMATION PER SERVING

Serving Size: 1 candy		Percent U.S. RDA	
Calories	80	Protein	*
Protein	1g	Vitamin A	*
Carbohydrate	11g	Vitamin C	*
Fat	5g	Thiamine	*
Cholesterol	0mg	Riboflavin	*
Sodium	0mg	Niacin	*
Potassium	70mg	Calcium	*
		Iron	2%
*Contains less than 2%			

Fruit and Nut Clusters

Praline Crunch

Praline Crunch

Irresistible Praline Crunch is a delightful gift all by itself. You'll also want to try this crunchy homemade confection in Praline Crunch Bark and Easy Praline Truffles.

Apricot-Raisin Brandy Balls

The flavor of these no-bake sweets improves with age. Store them in your freezer for a ready-to-serve holiday treat.

1 cup sugar
2 tablespoons butter
1 cup chopped pecans

Line cookie sheet with foil; lightly butter foil. In large heavy skillet, combine sugar and butter; cook over medium-high heat until sugar is melted and turns golden, about 5 minutes, stirring constantly. Add pecans; stir until pecans are lightly toasted and well coated with sugar mixture, about 1 minute. Quickly spread mixture evenly on buttered, foil-lined cookie sheet. Cool completely; break or chop into bite-size pieces. Store in airtight container. **2 cups.**

NUTRITION INFORMATION PER SERVING

Serving Size: 1 tablespoon		Percent U.S. RDA	
Calories	50	Protein	*
Protein	0g	Vitamin A	*
Carbohydrate	7g	Vitamin C	*
Fat	3g	Thiamine	*
Cholesterol	2mg	Riboflavin	*
Sodium	5mg	Niacin	*
Potassium	15mg	Calcium	*
		Iron	*
*Contains less than 2%			

Praline Crunch Bark

16 ounces vanilla-flavored candy coating, cut into pieces
1 cup Praline Crunch (above)

Line large cookie sheet with waxed paper. In large saucepan over low heat, melt vanilla coating, stirring constantly. Stir in Praline Crunch. Spread mixture on waxed paper-lined cookie sheet. Refrigerate until set. Break into pieces Store in airtight container in cool, dry place. **22 ounces.**

MICROWAVE DIRECTIONS: Line large cookie sheet with waxed paper. In 4-cup microwave-safe measuring cup, microwave vanilla coating on MEDIUM for 3 to 4 minutes, stirring once

halfway through cooking. Stir until smooth. Continue as directed above.

NUTRITION INFORMATION PER SERVING

Serving Size: 1 ounce		Percent U.S. RDA	
Calories	150	Protein	2%
Protein	1g	Vitamin A	*
Carbohydrate	18g	Vitamin C	*
Fat	9g	Thiamine	*
Cholesterol	6mg	Riboflavin	2%
Sodium	25mg	Niacin	*
Potassium	75mg	Calcium	4%
		Iron	*
*Contains less than 2%			

Apricot-Raisin Brandy Balls

½ cup golden raisins
½ cup chopped dried apricots
⅓ cup brandy
1 (12-ounce) package chocolate wafers
Unsweetened cocoa or powdered sugar

In small bowl, combine raisins, apricots and brandy. Let stand at room temperature for 1 hour. Meanwhile, in food processor bowl with metal blade, process wafers into crumbs. Add fruit mixture and process until well blended. Shape mixture into 1-inch balls. Roll in cocoa. Store in airtight container. **4 dozen candies.**

TIP: When food processor is unavailable, crush wafers with rolling pin to form crumbs. Snip raisins and apricots with scissors. In medium bowl, combine fruit mixture with wafer crumbs and stir until well blended.

NUTRITION INFORMATION PER SERVING

Serving Size: 1 candy		Percent U.S. RDA	
Calories	45	Protein	*
Protein	1g	Vitamin A	2%
Carbohydrate	8g	Vitamin C	*
Fat	1g	Thiamine	*
Cholesterol	3mg	Riboflavin	*
Sodium	10mg	Niacin	*
Potassium	40mg	Calcium	*
		Iron	*
*Contains less than 2%			

Easy Chocolate Truffles

1 (12-ounce) package vanilla milk chips or milk chocolate chips
¼ cup dairy sour cream
2 tablespoons Amaretto
Powdered sugar

Melt chips in small saucepan over low heat, stirring constantly. Remove from heat. Stir in sour cream and Amaretto; blend well. Refrigerate 30 to 60 minutes or until mixture is easy to handle. Using hands or melon baller, roll mixture into ¾-inch balls; roll in powdered sugar. Place in paper candy cups, if desired. Store in airtight container in refrigerator up to 4 weeks.
5 dozen candies.

MICROWAVE DIRECTIONS: In medium microwave-safe bowl, microwave chips on MEDIUM for 3 to 4 minutes, stirring once halfway through cooking. Stir until smooth. Continue as directed above.

TIPS: For variety, truffles can be rolled in finely chopped almonds. Truffles made using milk chocolate chips can be rolled in unsweetened cocoa, finely chopped nuts or chocolate sprinkles.

Truffles can be frozen in an airtight container.

NUTRITION INFORMATION PER SERVING

Serving Size: 1 candy		Percent U.S. RDA	
Calories	35	Protein	*
Protein	0g	Vitamin A	*
Carbohydrate	4g	Vitamin C	*
Fat	2g	Thiamine	*
Cholesterol	1mg	Riboflavin	*
Sodium	10mg	Niacin	*
Potassium	25mg	Calcium	*
		Iron	*
*Contains less than 2%			

Easy Praline Truffles

1 (12-ounce) package (2 cups) semi-sweet chocolate chips
¼ cup dairy sour cream
2 tablespoons praline liqueur
¾ cup finely chopped Praline Crunch*

Melt chocolate chips in small saucepan over low heat, stirring constantly. Remove from heat. Stir in sour cream and liqueur; blend well. Refrigerate 30 to 60 minutes or until mixture is easy to handle. Using hands or melon baller, roll mixture into ¾-inch balls; roll in Praline Crunch. Place in paper candy cups, if desired. Store in airtight container in refrigerator up to 4 weeks.
4 dozen candies.

MICROWAVE DIRECTIONS: In medium microwave-safe bowl, microwave chocolate chips on MEDIUM for 3 to 4 minutes, stirring once halfway through cooking. Stir until smooth. Continue as directed above.

TIPS: *Recipe for Praline Crunch is on page 38. Use a food processor to finely chop the bite-size pieces.

Truffles can be frozen in an airtight container.

NUTRITION INFORMATION PER SERVING

Serving Size: 1 candy		Percent U.S. RDA	
Calories	50	Protein	*
Protein	0g	Vitamin A	*
Carbohydrate	6g	Vitamin C	*
Fat	4g	Thiamine	*
Cholesterol	1mg	Riboflavin	*
Sodium	0mg	Niacin	*
Potassium	30mg	Calcium	*
		Iron	*
*Contains less than 2%			

Easy Chocolate Truffles

Truffles are the ultimate chocolate luxury. Our recipe has been streamlined to include fewer ingredients and microwave directions. For an attractive platter, make one recipe using the vanilla milk chips and one using the milk chocolate chips. Serve them in colorful foil candy cups.

Easy Praline Truffles

Moisture in melted chocolate can cause it to thicken or "seize." In this recipe the addition of sour cream provides more fat, which helps avoid the problem.

Long-Stemmed Cherries Supreme

Long-Stemmed Cherries Supreme

Long-Stemmed Cherries Supreme

Homemade chocolate-covered cherries — easy and impressive!

1 (10-ounce) jar maraschino
   cherries with stems, drained
2 tablespoons rum
FONDANT
⅓ cup sweetened condensed milk
   (not evaporated)
2 teaspoons light corn syrup
2¼ to 2½ cups powdered sugar

COATING
1 (12-ounce) package dipping
   chocolate*

In small bowl, combine cherries and rum. Let soak 2 hours; drain on paper towels.

In medium bowl, combine condensed milk and corn syrup; blend well. Add powdered sugar gradually, stirring until mixture forms a stiff smooth dough. (If all powdered sugar cannot be stirred in, knead mixture and sugar on counter until smooth dough forms.) Wrap small amount of fondant around each cherry to cover completely. Refrigerate about 20 minutes or until fondant is firm.

Line cookie sheet with waxed paper. In top of double boiler or in heavy saucepan over low heat, melt chocolate, stirring constantly. Holding by stem, dip chilled cherries into chocolate, making sure to cover completely. Place on waxed paper-lined cookie sheet; refrigerate until chocolate sets, about 10 minutes. Dip chilled candies into melted chocolate again, making sure to coat completely. Place on waxed paper-lined cookie sheet; cover loosely with waxed paper. Let stand several days in cool place to allow fondant to liquefy. (*Do not refrigerate.*) Store in airtight container in refrigerator.

2½ dozen candies.

TIP: *If dipping chocolate is unavailable, in heavy saucepan combine 1 (6-ounce) package (1 cup) semi-sweet chocolate chips, ¼ cup light corn syrup and 1 tablespoon water. Cook over low heat until melted, stirring occasionally. Dip and store as directed above.

NUTRITION INFORMATION PER SERVING

Serving Size: 1 candy		Percent U.S. RDA	
Calories	110	Protein	*
Protein	1g	Vitamin A	*
Carbohydrate	19g	Vitamin C	*
Fat	4g	Thiamine	*
Cholesterol	4mg	Riboflavin	2%
Sodium	15mg	Niacin	*
Potassium	50mg	Calcium	2%
		Iron	*
*Contains less than 2%			

Cherry Nougat Fudge Slices

NOUGAT

1 envelope unflavored gelatin
3 tablespoons water
¼ cup sugar
⅓ cup light corn syrup
1 teaspoon vanilla
2 to 2½ cups powdered sugar
½ cup chopped red candied cherries

CARAMEL

1 (14-ounce) package fudge-flavored caramels
2 tablespoons corn syrup
1 cup chopped toasted almonds*

MICROWAVE DIRECTIONS: On each of 3 sheets of waxed paper, generously butter an 8 × 4-inch rectangle. In small microwave-safe bowl, combine gelatin and water; let stand 5 minutes. Stir in sugar and ⅓ cup corn syrup. Microwave on HIGH for 2 to 2½ minutes or until mixture boils, stirring once halfway through cooking. Cool 5 minutes. Add vanilla. Beat on high speed until soft peaks form, 5 to 8 minutes. Stir in 1 cup of the powdered sugar and cherries. Gradually stir in ½ to ¾ cup powdered sugar. On surface sprinkled lightly with powdered sugar, knead in an additional ½ to ¾ cup powdered sugar until mixture is easy to handle and no longer sticky. Divide mixture into thirds. Shape each third into 8-inch log; set aside.

Place ⅓ of the caramels in small microwave-safe bowl. Microwave on HIGH for 20 to 40 seconds or until soft, stirring once halfway through cooking. *Do not melt.* On buttered waxed paper, press softened caramels into 8 × 4-inch rectangle. Place nougat log on center of rectangle; wrap caramel around log. Repeat with remaining nougat logs and caramels.

Brush logs with 2 tablespoons corn syrup. Roll logs in almonds. Wrap in waxed paper; refrigerate. To serve, cut crosswise into ½-inch slices. (Dip knife into hot water if necessary to minimize sticking.) Store candies between sheets of waxed paper in loosely covered container in cool dry place.

4 dozen candies.

TIP: *To toast almonds, spread in thin layer in microwave-safe pie pan. Microwave on HIGH for 5 to 7 minutes or until light golden brown, stirring frequently.

NUTRITION INFORMATION PER SERVING

Serving Size: 1 candy		Percent U.S. RDA	
Calories	90	Protein	*
Protein	1g	Vitamin A	*
Carbohydrate	17g	Vitamin C	*
Fat	2g	Thiamine	*
Cholesterol	0mg	Riboflavin	2%
Sodium	20mg	Niacin	*
Potassium	35mg	Calcium	2%
		Iron	*
		*Contains less than 2%	

Chocolate-Dipped Nuts

1 ounce (1 square) semi-sweet chocolate
1 cup whole almonds, walnut halves or pecan halves

Line cookie sheets with waxed paper. In small saucepan over low heat, melt chocolate. Set saucepan in hot water to maintain dipping consistency. Dip 1 end of each nut in melted chocolate. Place on waxed paper-lined cookie sheets. Refrigerate until set. Place in paper candy cups. Cover; store in refrigerator.

1 cup.

NUTRITION INFORMATION PER SERVING

Serving Size: 2 tablespoons		Percent U.S. RDA	
		Protein	6%
Calories	120	Vitamin A	*
Protein	4g	Vitamin C	*
Carbohydrate	6g	Thiamine	2%
Fat	11g	Riboflavin	8%
Cholesterol	0mg	Niacin	2%
Sodium	0mg	Calcium	4%
Potassium	140mg	Iron	4%
		*Contains less than 2%	

Cherry Nougat Fudge Slices

This colorful candy takes a bit more time to prepare but is certainly worth the effort!

Chocolate-Dipped Nuts

Serve these dipped treats on your cookie and candy tray, or use them to garnish that extra-special dessert.

Sugared Citrus Strips

Sugared Citrus Strips

Tart and tangy candies made from the peel of grapefruit or oranges.

Microwave Chunky Peanut Butter Cups

This recipe is sure to become a family favorite. The miniature paper baking cups are available at kitchen specialty shops.

2 large grapefruit or 3 large
  oranges
  Cold water
3 cups sugar
1 cup water

Remove peel from fruit in long continuous strips; cut into 1/4 × 1 1/2-inch pieces. In medium saucepan, cover peel with cold water. Bring to a boil and cook until tender, pouring off water and adding fresh cold water several times; drain. Remove peel from water. With spoon, remove white inner portion of peel.

In medium saucepan, combine 2 cups of the sugar, 1 cup water and peel.* Cook over low heat until peel appears candied and almost transparent. Remove peel 2 or 3 strips at a time; allow excess syrup to drain back into saucepan. Roll citrus strips in remaining 1 cup sugar until well coated. Place on wire rack; let dry about 4 hours. Store in airtight container.
8 to 10 ounces.

TIP: *If desired, add a few drops green food color to syrup when making sugared grapefruit peel.

NUTRITION INFORMATION: Variables in this recipe make it impossible to calculate nutrition information.

Microwave Chunky Peanut Butter Cups

FILLING
3/4 cup chunky peanut butter
1/2 cup powdered sugar

COATING
1 1/2 cups chocolate chips
9 ounces chocolate-flavored candy
  coating, cut into pieces
2/3 cup chunky peanut butter
  Miniature paper baking cups
  (1-inch diameter)

MICROWAVE DIRECTIONS: In small bowl, combine filling ingredients; stir until mixture forms a ball. Refrigerate 1 hour for easier handling. Shape 1/2 teaspoonfuls of mixture into balls. Place on sheet of waxed paper.

In medium microwave-safe bowl or 2-quart round casserole, microwave chocolate chips and chocolate coating on MEDIUM for 4 to 5 minutes, stirring twice. Stir until smooth. Add 2/3 cup peanut butter; blend well. Place about 1/2 teaspoonful of chocolate-peanut butter mixture in each paper baking cup; top each with peanut butter ball. Fill cups with remaining chocolate-peanut butter mixture.* Refrigerate 30 minutes or until set.
6 dozen candies.

CONVENTIONAL DIRECTIONS: Prepare filling as directed above. In small saucepan over low heat, melt chocolate chips and chocolate coating, stirring constantly. Stir in 2/3 cup peanut butter; blend well. Continue as directed above.

TIP: *If mixture becomes too stiff, microwave on MEDIUM for 20 to 30 seconds to soften.

NUTRITION INFORMATION PER SERVING

Serving Size: 1 candy		Percent U.S. RDA	
Calories	80	Protein	2%
Protein	2g	Vitamin A	*
Carbohydrate	7g	Vitamin C	*
Fat	6g	Thiamine	*
Cholesterol	1mg	Riboflavin	*
Sodium	35mg	Niacin	4%
Potassium	70mg	Calcium	*
		Iron	*
		*Contains less than 2%	

Taffy

1½ cups sugar
2 cups light corn syrup
¼ cup margarine or butter
½ teaspoon salt
2 teaspoons vanilla

Grease 15 × 10 × 1-inch baking pan. In large saucepan, combine sugar and corn syrup. Bring to a boil, stirring constantly. Add margarine; stir until melted. Cook, without stirring, until candy thermometer reaches 260°. (hard-ball stage). Remove from heat; stir in salt and vanilla. Pour into greased pan. Cool slightly; fold edges toward center to cool evenly.

When taffy is just cool enough to handle, divide into 4 or 5 pieces. With buttered hands, pull and fold taffy for 10 to 20 minutes or until taffy turns opaque and stiff.* Pull into long rope about ½ inch wide and cut into 1-inch pieces while stil warm. Wrap individual pieces in waxed paper and store in cool, dry place.
1½ pounds.

TIP: *If candy becomes too stiff to work with, warm briefly in oven at 350°F.

NUTRITION INFORMATION PER SERVING

Serving Size: 1 ounce		Percent U.S. RDA	
Calories	140	Protein	*
Protein	0g	Vitamin A	*
Carbohydrate	33g	Vitamin C	*
Fat	2g	Thiamine	*
Cholesterol	0mg	Riboflavin	*
Sodium	85mg	Niacin	*
Potassium	0mg	Calcium	*
		Iron	6%
		*Contains less than 2%	

Candied Pecans

1 cup firmly packed brown sugar
⅓ cup orange juice
4 cups pecan halves

Heat oven to 350°F. Butter 15 × 10 × 1-inch baking pan; butter sheet of foil or waxed paper. In medium bowl, combine brown sugar and orange juice; blend well. Add pecans; toss to coat. Spread on buttered pan. Bake at 350°F. for 10 to 13 minutes or until bubbly and dark golden brown, stirring occasionally. Immediately spread on buttered foil. Cool completely; break apart.
18 ounces (2 cups).

MICROWAVE DIRECTIONS: Butter 12 × 8-inch (2-quart) microwave-safe dish; butter sheet of foil or waxed paper. In medium bowl, combine brown sugar and orange juice; blend well. Add pecans; toss to coat. Spread in buttered dish. Microwave on HIGH for 6 to 8 minutes or until bubbly and dark golden brown, stirring every 2 minutes. Immediately spread on buttered foil. Cool completely; break apart.

NUTRITION INFORMATION PER SERVING

Serving Size: 1 ounce		Percent U.S. RDA	
Calories	210	Protein	2%
Protein	2g	Vitamin A	*
Carbohydrate	18g	Vitamin C	4%
Fat	16g	Thiamine	4%
Cholesterol	0mg	Riboflavin	*
Sodium	0mg	Niacin	*
Potassium	140mg	Calcium	*
		Iron	4%
		*Contains less than 2%	

Taffy

Candy making, especially an old-fashioned taffy pull, is an enjoyable group activity. Invite family and friends to join in the fun.

Candied Pecans

These crunchy orange-and-praline-flavored nuts will be one of the joys of the season.

Holiday Bread Basket

Sweet & Savory Breads
for Breakfast, Lunch or Dinner

From Thanksgiving through the festivities of New Year's Day, occasions abound to break — and even make — bread with family and friends.

During this season of celebration, everyday breads, rolls, coffee cakes and muffins don their holiday finery: nuts, raisins, spices, glazes, candied cherries, and intricate shapes. These out-of-the-ordinary breads appear at breakfasts, brunches, lunches and dinners as well as on buffet tables, in gift baskets, and on snack trays during breaks from a stint of gift wrapping.

Many of these holiday breads have their roots in traditions stretching back through generations and carried to America from foreign homelands. What better time than during the holidays to share and pass down to the young ones the stories of Great-Great Grandmother's *Julekake*, Great-Aunt's Rustic Oats and Wheat Bread or Mother's Santa Lucia Buns? In this chapter you'll find recipes for these ethnic breads, often in updated versions that make their preparation simpler during the rush-rush of the season or any time of the year. For instance, Hungry Jack® Lefse is made with mashed potato flakes and Tannebaum Dinner Rolls begin with refrigerated soft breadsticks.

Other breads are pretty enough to be centerpieces for the table: Cherry Twist Coffee Cake with its distinctive pinwheel shape; Partridge Bread with Orange-Honey Butter, a dramatic bird-shaped loaf that needs only a pear tree to be complete; and Whole Wheat Pull-Apart Wreaths bedecked with fruit-leather ribbons and bows.

To accompany these beautiful breads or to round out a gift basket, include a jar of Harvest Fruit Conserve, Orange-Cream Cheese Spread, Cran-Apple Spiced Jelly or Fresh Citrus Curd. All of these go-alongs are short on ingredients and long on easy fixing. Try serving the conserve with thick, warm slices of multigrain bread or the cream cheese spread with Texas-sized Praline Pumpkin Date Muffins. The citrus curd complements pound cake as well as scones, and dollops of the spiced jelly top a quick crackers and cream cheese hors d'oeuvre.

Partridge Bread with Orange-Honey Butter

BREAD
1 package hot roll mix
2 tablespoons sugar
1 tablespoon grated orange peel
Juice of 1 orange plus water to make 1 cup liquid*
1 teaspoon almond extract
1 egg, slightly beaten

ORANGE-HONEY BUTTER
½ cup butter or margarine, softened
¼ cup honey
1 teaspoon grated orange peel

GARNISH
3 tablespoons sliced almonds
Powdered sugar

In large bowl, combine flour mixture with yeast from foil packet, 2 tablespoons sugar and 1 tablespoon orange peel; blend well. In small saucepan, heat orange juice liquid until very warm (120 to 130°F.). Stir in orange juice liquid, almond extract and egg until dough pulls away from sides of bowl. Turn dough out onto floured surface. With greased or floured hands, shape dough into a ball. Knead dough 5 minutes until smooth. Divide dough into 2 equal pieces. Cover with large bowl; let rest 5 minutes.

Grease large cookie sheet. On floured surface, using rolling pin or hands, shape 1 piece of dough into 8 × 4-inch oval forming the wings of the bird. Place crosswise in center of greased cookie sheet. Shape second piece into triangle 12 inches high and 6 inches across the bottom. Center triangle lengthwise over oval. Twist and turn over narrow end of triangle to the right, forming head. Pinch point to form beak. Twist and turn over wide end of triangle to the left for tail; make five 1-inch cuts across bottom and separate to form tail feathers. (See diagram.) Cover dough with plastic wrap and cloth towel. Let rise in warm place (80 to 85°F.) until light and doubled in size, about 15 to 20 minutes.

Heat oven to 350°F. Uncover dough. Bake at 350°F. for 20 to 25 minutes or until golden brown and loaf sounds hollow when lightly tapped. Meanwhile, in small bowl combine orange-honey butter ingredients; beat until smooth. Remove bread from oven; brush with orange-honey butter. Arrange almonds on wings. Return to oven and bake an additional 5 minutes. Remove from cookie sheet; cool on wire rack. Sprinkle with powdered sugar. Serve with remaining orange-honey butter.
1 (16-slice) loaf.

TIP: *One-third cup orange juice concentrate plus ⅔ cup water can be substituted for fresh orange juice.

HIGH ALTITUDE—Above 3500 Feet: No change.

NUTRITION INFORMATION PER SERVING
Serving Size: 1 slice

		Percent U.S. RDA	
Calories	190		
Protein	4g	Protein	6%
Carbohydrate	28g	Vitamin A	4%
Fat	7g	Vitamin C	4%
Cholesterol	29mg	Thiamine	10%
Sodium	260mg	Riboflavin	10%
Potassium	65mg	Niacin	8%
		Calcium	*
		Iron	6%

*Contains less than 2%

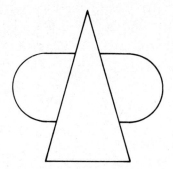

Diagrams for Partridge Bread

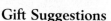
Pictured on preceding pages: Partridge Bread with Orange-Honey Butter

Praline Pumpkin Date Muffins

Praline Pumpkin
Date Muffins

MUFFINS
1 package date bread mix*
½ cup canned pumpkin
½ cup water
¼ cup oil
1 egg
½ cup chopped pecans
1 teaspoon cinnamon
⅛ teaspoon cloves

TOPPING
⅓ cup firmly packed brown sugar
⅓ cup chopped pecans
1 tablespoon margarine or butter, softened

Heat oven to 350°F. Grease 6 jumbo-size muffin cups or line with jumbo-size paper baking cups.** In large bowl, combine all muffin ingredients; stir by hand 50 to 75 strokes or until dry particles are moistened. Divide batter evenly among muffin cups. In small bowl, combine all topping ingredients; sprinkle evenly over batter.

Bake at 350°F. for 30 to 40 minutes or until toothpick inserted in center comes out clean. Cool 15 minutes; remove from pan. Cool completely on wire rack. Wrap tightly and store in refrigerator.

6 jumbo-size muffins.

TIPS: *If desired, substitute nut bread mix and omit pecans in muffins. Decrease baking time 5 minutes.

**Each jumbo-size muffin cup is about ⅔ cup. To make standard-size muffins, line 12 muffin cups with paper baking cups. Divide batter evenly among muffin cups and bake at 400°F. for 20 to 25 minutes. 12 muffins.

HIGH ALTITUDE — Above 3500 Feet: Add 2 tablespoons flour to dry bread mix. Bake as directed above.

NUTRITION INFORMATION PER SERVING

Serving Size: 1 jumbo-size muffin		Percent U.S. RDA	
		Protein	10%
Calories	570	Vitamin A	90%
Protein	6g	Vitamin C	*
Carbohydrate	81g	Thiamine	15%
Fat	25g	Riboflavin	10%
Cholesterol	35mg	Niacin	10%
Sodium	320mg	Calcium	6%
Potassium	280mg	Iron	15%
		*Contains less than 2%	

COOK'S NOTE

Muffins

Although it's tempting to overmix muffin batter, for light, tender muffins combine just until dry ingredients are moistened. Overmixing causes peaked tops and a tough, tunneled texture. For good-looking muffins, set the oven temperature accurately and fill muffin cups with batter to the level the recipe directs.

Rum Raisin
Swirl Loaf

Rum Raisin Swirl Loaf

Made with hot roll mix, this frosted bread would also make a great gift.

Fresh Citrus Curd

A traditional English preserve to serve with scones, muffins or toast. Makes enough to give a jar to a friend.

FILLING
- ½ cup raisins
- ¼ cup rum*
- ¼ cup firmly packed brown sugar
- 2 tablespoons margarine or butter, softened

BREAD
- 1 package hot roll mix
- 1 cup water heated to 120 to 130°F.
- 2 tablespoons margarine or butter, softened
- 1 egg

FROSTING
- 1 cup powdered sugar
- ¼ teaspoon rum extract
- 1 to 2 tablespoons milk

Grease 9 × 5-inch loaf pan. In small saucepan, combine raisins and rum; heat several minutes or until raisins absorb rum. Remove from heat; cool. Set aside. In small bowl, combine brown sugar and 2 tablespoons margarine; beat until smooth. Set aside.

In large bowl, combine flour mixture with yeast from foil packet; blend well. Stir in *hot* water, 2 tablespoons margarine and egg until dough pulls away from sides of bowl. Turn dough out onto lightly floured surface. With greased or floured hands, shape dough into a ball. Knead dough 5 minutes until smooth. Cover with large bowl; let rest 5 minutes.

Roll dough into 14 × 7-inch rectangle. Spread dough with brown sugar mixture; sprinkle with raisins. Starting with shorter side, roll up tightly, pressing edges to seal. Place seam side down in greased pan; cover loosely with plastic wrap and cloth towel. Let rise in warm place (80 to 85°F.) until light and doubled in size, about 30 minutes.

Heat oven to 375°F. Uncover dough. Bake at 375°F. for 30 to 40 minutes or until loaf sounds hollow when lightly tapped. Immediately remove from pan; cool on wire rack.

In small bowl, combine all frosting ingredients, adding enough milk for desired spreading consistency. Frost cooled loaf.

1 (16-slice) loaf.

TIP: *One-fourth cup water and 1 teaspoon rum extract can be substituted for rum.

HIGH ALTITUDE—Above 3500 Feet: Decrease rise time to 20 to 25 minutes. Bake as directed above.

NUTRITION INFORMATION PER SERVING

Serving Size: 1 slice		Percent U.S. RDA	
Calories	190	Protein	6%
Protein	4g	Vitamin A	2%
Carbohydrate	34g	Vitamin C	*
Fat	4g	Thiamine	10%
Cholesterol	13mg	Riboflavin	10%
Sodium	230mg	Niacin	8%
Potassium	95mg	Calcium	*
		Iron	6%
		*Contains less than 2%	

Fresh Citrus Curd

- 1 medium lemon
- 1 medium orange
- 1½ cups sugar
- ¾ cup margarine or butter
- 4 eggs, beaten

Grate peel from lemon and orange; squeeze ¼ cup juice from each. In heavy 2-quart saucepan, combine lemon juice, orange juice, sugar and margarine. Cook over low heat until margarine is melted. Gradually stir in eggs, stirring constantly. Cook over low heat, stirring constantly, until mixture boils and thickens, about 20 minutes. Add lemon and orange peel; blend well. Cool slightly. Ladle into clean jars or nonmetal containers; cover with tight-fitting lids. Store in refrigerator up to 2 weeks.

3 cups.

NUTRITION INFORMATION PER SERVING

Serving Size: 1 tablespoon		Percent U.S. RDA	
		Protein	*
Calories	60	Vitamin A	2%
Protein	1g	Vitamin C	*
Carbohydrate	7g	Thiamine	*
Fat	3g	Riboflavin	*
Cholesterol	18mg	Niacin	*
Sodium	40mg	Calcium	*
Potassium	10mg	Iron	*
		*Contains less than 2%	

Cranberry Scone Loaf; Fresh Citrus Curd

Cranberry Scone Loaf

1 package cranberry bread mix
⅔ cup dairy sour cream
⅓ cup milk
1 egg
1 egg, separated, reserving egg
　white for topping
1 tablespoon sugar

Heat oven to 400°F. Grease and flour bottom only of 9-inch pie pan. In large bowl, combine bread mix, sour cream, milk, 1 whole egg and 1 egg yolk; stir 50 to 75 strokes until dry particles are moistened. Spread in greased and floured pan. In small bowl, slightly beat reserved egg white; brush over top of batter. Sprinkle evenly with sugar.

Bake at 400°F. for 25 to 30 minutes or until golden brown and toothpick inserted in center comes out clean. Serve warm, cut into wedges.

1 (8-wedge) loaf.

HIGH ALTITUDE — Above 3500 Feet: Add 1 tablespoon flour to dry bread mix. Bake as directed above.

NUTRITION INFORMATION PER SERVING

Serving Size: ⅛ of recipe		Percent U.S. RDA	
		Protein	8%
Calories	280	Vitamin A	4%
Protein	6g	Vitamin C	2%
Carbohydrate	49g	Thiamine	10%
Fat	8g	Riboflavin	10%
Cholesterol	63mg	Niacin	8%
Sodium	260mg	Calcium	6%
Potassium	100mg	Iron	6%
		*Contains less than 2%	

Cranberry Scone Loaf

Served with Fresh Citrus Curd, this simple-to-make coffee bread is great for breakfast or brunch.

Tannenbaum Dinner Rolls

Tannenbaum Dinner Rolls

Tannenbaum, *the German word for pine tree, is an apt name for these easy-to-shape dinner rolls.*

Santa Lucia Buns

Swedish households celebrate St. Lucia Day on December thirteenth to mark the beginning of the Christmas season, and the oldest daughter often serves the dinner. Traditional Santa Lucia buns are made with yeast dough flavored with saffron. Our quick and easy version uses refrigerated breadsticks and is glazed with honey butter.

ROLLS
1 (11-ounce) can refrigerated soft breadsticks

HONEY BUTTER
½ cup unsalted butter, regular butter or margarine, softened
¼ cup honey

Heat oven to 350°F. Lightly grease cookie sheet. Remove breadsticks from can and separate into 8 pieces. To shape trees, unroll each breadstick into a 12-inch rope. Cut a 4-inch, a 3-inch, a 2-inch and two 1½-inch pieces from each breadstick. Roll 8 of the 1½-inch pieces into small balls. As shown in diagram, assemble pieces with edges touching, forming 8 trees. Bake at 350°F. for 15 minutes.

Meanwhile, in small bowl combine butter and honey; beat until light and fluffy. Remove rolls from oven and brush with honey butter. Bake an additional 2 to 3 minutes or until golden brown. Serve warm with remaining honey butter.

8 rolls.

NUTRITION INFORMATION PER SERVING

Serving Size: 1 roll		Percent U.S. RDA	
Calories	240	Protein	4%
Protein	3g	Vitamin A	8%
Carbohydrate	25g	Vitamin C	*
Fat	14g	Thiamine	100%
Cholesterol	31mg	Riboflavin	6%
Sodium	230mg	Niacin	6%
Potassium	35mg	Calcium	*
		Iron	6%
		*Contains less than 2%	

Santa Lucia Buns

BUNS
1 (11-ounce) can refrigerated soft breadsticks
16 raisins
1 egg, beaten

HONEY BUTTER
½ cup unsalted butter, regular butter or margarine, softened
¼ cup honey

Heat oven to 350°F. Lightly grease cookie sheets. Remove breadsticks from can and separate into 8 pieces. Unroll each breadstick into a 12-inch rope. To form "S"-shaped buns, coil ends of rope making an "S" shape. To form "X"-shaped buns, cross 2 dough ropes to form "X" shape; coil each end counterclockwise. To form wagon wheel-shaped bun, place 2 dough pieces side by side; coil each end. (See diagram.) Press raisin in center of each coil. Lightly brush dough with beaten egg. Bake at 350°F. for 15 minutes.

Meanwhile, in small bowl combine butter and honey; beat until light and fluffy. Remove buns from oven and brush with honey butter. Bake an additional 2 to 3 minutes or until golden brown. Serve warm with remaining honey butter.

8 buns.

NUTRITION INFORMATION PER SERVING

Serving Size: 1 bun		Percent U.S. RDA	
Calories	250	Protein	6%
Protein	4g	Vitamin A	8%
Carbohydrate	26g	Vitamin C	*
Fat	15g	Thiamine	100%
Cholesterol	58mg	Riboflavin	8%
Sodium	240mg	Niacin	6%
Potassium	45mg	Calcium	*
		Iron	6%
		*Contains less than 2%	

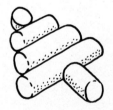

Diagram for Tannenbaum Dinner Rolls

Diagrams for Santa Lucia Buns

Anise Rolls

1 package active dry yeast
¼ cup water heated to 110 to 120°F.
1 cup milk
6 tablespoons margarine or butter
¼ cup sugar
1 teaspoon salt
1 teaspoon anise seed
1 egg
3 to 4 cups all purpose flour or unbleached flour

In large bowl, dissolve yeast in warm water. In small saucepan, heat milk, margarine, sugar, salt and anise seed until warm (110 to 120°F.). Add warm liquid and egg to yeast; blend well. Lightly spoon flour into measuring cup; level off. Add 1½ cups flour to liquid mixture. By hand, beat until smooth. Stir in remaining 1½ to 2½ cups flour to make a soft dough. Cover loosely with plastic wrap and cloth towel. Let rise in warm place (80 to 85°F.) until light and doubled in size, about 1 hour.

Stir down dough to remove all air bubbles. Cover with greased plastic wrap and cloth towel; let rise in warm place until light, about 30 minutes. With floured hands, shape heaping tablespoonful of dough into 8-inch rope; shape into figure 8, sealing ends and tucking underneath. Place on ungreased cookie sheet. Repeat for remaining rolls. Cover; let rise in warm place about 30 minutes or until doubled in size.

Heat oven to 400°F. Uncover dough. Bake at 400°F. for 12 to 15 minutes or until golden brown. Remove from cookie sheets; cool on wire rack.
30 rolls.

HIGH ALTITUDE — Above 3500 Feet: No change.

NUTRITION INFORMATION PER SERVING

Serving Size: 1 roll		Percent U.S. RDA	
Calories	90	Protein	2%
Protein	2g	Vitamin A	2%
Carbohydrate	15g	Vitamin C	*
Fat	3g	Thiamine	8%
Cholesterol	8mg	Riboflavin	6%
Sodium	105mg	Niacin	4%
Potassium	40mg	Calcium	*
		Iron	4%
*Contains less than 2%			

Hungry Jack® Lefse

3 cups mashed potato flakes
1 cup water
2 tablespoons butter or margarine
2 teaspoons salt
1 cup milk
¾ to 1 cup all purpose or unbleached flour
Butter or margarine

Heat electric *lefse* griddle or electric skillet to highest temperature setting. *Do not grease griddle or skillet.* Place potato flakes in large bowl. In small saucepan, combine water, butter and salt; bring to a boil. Remove from heat; add milk. Add liquid all at once to potato flakes, stirring until all flakes are moistened. (Mixture will be crumbly.) Gradually add flour to potato mixture, working with hands until a soft dough forms and is of rolling consistency. (Avoid adding too much flour.) Form dough into a roll 10 inches long and about 2 inches in diameter. Cut roll into ½-inch slices. Cover with plastic wrap while rolling out each *lefse*.

Using stockinette-covered rolling pin and well-floured pastry cloth, roll out 1 slice of dough at a time until paper-thin. Transfer to heated griddle, using *lefse* stick or long spatula. Bake until brown spots appear on bottom surface, about 1 minute. Turn and bake other side about 30 to 45 seconds. Place baked *lefse* between cloth towels to prevent drying. Repeat with remaining slices, flouring rolling pin and cloth before rolling out each *lefse*. Cool completely. To serve, spread with butter; fold into quarters or cut into wedges and roll up.
20 lefse.

NUTRITION INFORMATION PER SERVING

Serving Size: 1 lefse		Percent U.S. RDA	
Calories	100	Protein	2%
Protein	2g	Vitamin A	4%
Carbohydrate	12g	Vitamin C	*
Fat	5g	Thiamine	2%
Cholesterol	14mg	Riboflavin	2%
Sodium	280mg	Niacin	4%
Potassium	95mg	Calcium	2%
		Iron	2%
*Contains less than 2%			

Anise Rolls

The mild anise flavor lends an Old World touch to these easy-to-make dinner rolls. If you choose, shape them into family members' initials.

Hungry Jack® Lefse

Potato flakes simplify the preparation of this unleavened Scandinavian specialty served as an alternative to bread.

Cranberry-Orange Crescent Wreath

Cranberry-Orange Crescent Wreath

Cranberry-Orange Crescent Wreath

Use refrigerated crescent rolls and cranberry-orange relish to make a tasty holiday coffee cake.

BREAD
¼ cup frozen cranberry-orange relish, thawed, well drained, reserving 1 teaspoon liquid
⅛ teaspoon cinnamon
1 (8-ounce) can refrigerated crescent dinner rolls

GLAZE
¼ cup powdered sugar
Reserved 1 teaspoon cranberry-orange relish liquid
½ to 1½ teaspoons water

Heat oven to 375°F. Grease cookie sheet. In small bowl, combine cranberry-orange relish and cinnamon. Separate dough into triangles. Spread each triangle with 1 teaspoon relish mixture. Roll up each, starting with shortest side of triangle and rolling to opposite point; curve to form crescent shape with point underneath. Place crescents, points side down, side by side in a circle with ends pointing outward on greased cookie sheet. Bake at 375°F. for 11 to 16 minutes or until golden brown. Cool slightly; carefully remove from cookie sheet.

In small bowl, combine all glaze ingredients, adding enough water for desired drizzling consistency. Drizzle over warm coffee cake. Garnish as desired. **8 servings.**

NUTRITION INFORMATION PER SERVING

Serving Size: ⅛ of recipe		Percent U.S. RDA	
Calories	130	Protein	2%
Protein	2g	Vitamin A	*
Carbohydrate	18g	Vitamin C	*
Fat	6g	Thiamine	6%
Cholesterol	3mg	Riboflavin	2%
Sodium	240mg	Niacin	4%
Potassium	65mg	Calcium	*
		Iron	4%

*Contains less than 2%

Whole Wheat Pull-Apart Wreaths

4 to 5 cups all purpose or unbleached flour
¼ cup sugar
2 packages active dry yeast
1 teaspoon salt
1 cup milk
½ cup water
1 cup margarine or butter
2 eggs
2 cups whole wheat flour

GLAZE
1 egg
1 tablespoon water

GARNISH
2 red chewy fruit rolls*

Lightly spoon flour into measuring cup; level off. In large bowl, combine 2 cups all purpose flour, sugar, yeast and salt; blend well. In medium saucepan, heat milk, ½ cup water and margarine until very warm (120 to 130°F.). Add warm liquid and 2 eggs to flour mixture. Blend at low speed until moistened; beat 3 minutes at medium speed. By hand, stir in whole wheat flour and an additional 1¾ to 2¼ cups all purpose flour until dough pulls away from sides of bowl. On floured surface, knead in remaining ¼ to ¾ cup all purpose flour until dough is smooth and elastic, about 5 minutes. Place dough in greased bowl; cover loosely with plastic wrap and cloth towel. Let rise in warm place (80 to 85°F.) until light and doubled in size, about 35 to 45 minutes.

Grease 2 cookie sheets and outsides of two 6-ounce (4-inch) custard cups. Place 1 custard cup upside down in center of each greased cookie sheet. Punch down dough several times to remove all air bubbles. Divide dough into 4 equal parts. Roll each into 15-inch rope. Cut each rope into 15 pieces; shape into balls. On cookie sheets, form a circle around each custard cup with 8 balls of dough. Form a second circle around first ring with 12 balls. Lastly, form a ring of 10 balls on top of first and second circles.

In small bowl, combine glaze ingredients. Carefully brush wreaths with glaze. Cover with greased plastic wrap and cloth towel. Let rise in warm place until light and doubled in size, about 45 minutes.

Heat oven to 350°F. Carefully brush wreaths again with glaze. Bake at 350°F. for 25 to 30 minutes or until golden brown. Remove from oven; carefully remove custard cups. Remove breads from cookie sheets; cool on wire racks. Decorate with ribbon, bows, stars and/or other shapes cut from fruit rolls.

2 (15-slice) breads.

TIP: *Fruit rolls are also known as fruit leather.

ALTITUDE—Above 3500 Feet: No change.

NUTRITION INFORMATION PER SERVING

Serving Size: 1 slice		Percent U.S. RDA	
Calories	180	Protein	6%
Protein	4g	Vitamin A	6%
Carbohydrate	25g	Vitamin C	*
Fat	7g	Thiamine	15%
Cholesterol	22mg	Riboflavin	10%
Sodium	150mg	Niacin	10%
Potassium	90mg	Calcium	2%
		Iron	8%
		*Contains less than 2%	

Cranberry Spread

Serve this delicious creamy pink spread with a Whole Wheat Pull-Apart Wreath. Double the recipe if you're serving both wreaths for one occasion.

Cranberry Spread

1 (3-ounce) package cream cheese, softened
½ cup powdered sugar
¼ cup margarine or butter, softened
1 teaspoon vanilla
¼ cup chopped fresh or frozen cranberries

In small bowl, beat cream cheese, powdered sugar, margarine and vanilla until light and fluffy. Stir in cranberries. Store in refrigerator.

¾ cup.

NUTRITION INFORMATION PER SERVING

Serving Size: 1 tablespoon		Percent U.S. RDA	
		Protein	*
Calories	80	Vitamin A	4%
Protein	1g	Vitamin C	*
Carbohydrate	5g	Thiamine	*
Fat	6g	Riboflavin	*
Cholesterol	8mg	Niacin	*
Sodium	65mg	Calcium	*
Potassium	10mg	Iron	*
		*Contains less than 2%	

Honey Almond Twist

Honey Almond Twist

The honey almond glaze on these beautiful coffee cakes is the perfect finishing touch.

BREAD
6 to 7 cups bread flour*
½ cup sugar
2 teaspoons salt
2 packages active dry yeast
1 cup water
1 cup milk
½ cup margarine or butter
1 egg

FILLING
⅓ cup sugar
1 teaspoon cinnamon
3 tablespoons margarine or butter, softened

GLAZE
¼ cup sugar
¼ cup honey
2 tablespoons margarine or butter
½ cup slivered almonds

Grease 2 cookie sheets. Lightly spoon flour into measuring cup; level off. In large bowl, combine 2 cups flour, ½ cup sugar, salt and yeast; blend well. In small saucepan, heat water, milk and ½ cup margarine until very warm (120 to 130°F.). Add warm liquid and egg to flour mixture. Blend at low speed until moistened; beat 3 minutes at medium speed. By hand, stir in an additional 3 cups flour until dough pulls away from sides of bowl. On floured surface, knead in remaining 1 to 2 cups flour until dough is smooth and elastic with blisters under the surface, about 10 minutes. Place dough in greased bowl; cover loosely with plastic wrap and cloth towel. Let rise in warm place (80 to 85°F.) until light and doubled in size, about 1 hour.

Punch down dough several times to remove all air bubbles. Allow dough to rest on counter covered with inverted bowl for 15 minutes. In small bowl, combine ⅓ cup sugar and cinnamon; set aside. Divide dough into 3 equal pieces. On lightly floured surface, roll each piece of dough to 25 × 6-inch rectangle. Spread each with 1 tablespoon margarine. Sprinkle with sugar-cinnamon mixture. Starting with longer side, roll up tightly; pinch edges to seal. Twist each roll, stretching slightly. Form into pretzel shape; tuck ends under to seal. Place on greased cookie sheets. Cover; let rise in warm place until doubled in size, about 45 minutes.

Heat oven to 350°F. Uncover dough. Bake at 350°F. for 20 to 30 minutes or until deep golden brown. Immediately remove from cookie sheets; place on wire racks. In small saucepan, combine all glaze ingredients. Bring to a boil, stirring constantly. Spoon hot glaze over warm breads, completely covering tops and sides.

3 (16-slice) coffee cakes.

TIP: *All purpose or unbleached flour can be substituted for bread flour. Decrease kneading time to 5 minutes, omit resting period and decrease each rise time 15 minutes.

HIGH ALTITUDE — Above 3500 Feet: Decrease each rise time 15 minutes. Bake as directed above.

NUTRITION INFORMATION PER SERVING

Serving Size: 1 slice		Percent U.S. RDA	
Calories	140	Protein	4%
Protein	3g	Vitamin A	2%
Carbohydrate	21g	Vitamin C	*
Fat	4g	Thiamine	10%
Cholesterol	5mg	Riboflavin	8%
Sodium	130mg	Niacin	8%
Potassium	50mg	Calcium	*
		Iron	6%
		*Contains less than 2%	

Honey Almond Twist

Braided Holiday Stollen

BREAD
5½ to 6½ cups all purpose or
    unbleached flour
1 cup sugar
1 teaspoon salt
2 packages active dry yeast
1 cup water
1 cup milk
1 cup margarine or butter
2 eggs
1½ cups golden raisins
1½ cups slivered almonds

FROSTING
½ cup powdered sugar
2 teaspoons milk

Lightly spoon flour into measuring cup; level off. In large bowl, combine 2 cups flour, sugar, salt and yeast. In small saucepan, heat water, 1 cup milk and margarine until warm (105 to 115°F.). Add warm liquid and eggs to flour mixture. Blend at low speed until moistened; beat 2 minutes at medium speed. Stir in raisins, almonds and remaining 3½ to 4½ cups flour until dough pulls away from sides of bowl. Cover tightly and refrigerate overnight.

When ready to bake, grease 3 cookie sheets. Remove dough from refrigerator. On lightly floured surface, divide dough into 3 equal parts. Divide each part into 3 pieces. Roll each piece into a rope 16 inches long. Place 3 ropes lengthwise on each greased cookie sheet. Braid ropes loosely from center to each end. Pinch ends together; tuck under to seal. Cover; let rise in warm place (80 to 85°F.) until doubled in size, about 1½ to 2 hours.

Heat oven to 350°F. Uncover dough. Bake at 350°F. for 25 to 35 minutes or until light golden brown.* Immediately remove from cookie sheets; cool on wire racks. In small bowl, combine frosting ingredients. Drizzle over cooled loaves.
3 (16-slice) loaves.

TIP: *If baking only 1 loaf at a time, cover and refrigerate remaining loaves until ready to bake. If baking 2 loaves, alternate cookie sheet positions in oven halfway through baking.

HIGH ALTITUDE — Above 3500 Feet: No change.

NUTRITION INFORMATION PER SERVING

Serving Size: 1 slice		Percent U.S. RDA	
Calories	160	Protein	4%
Protein	3g	Vitamin A	2%
Carbohydrate	23g	Vitamin C	*
Fat	7g	Thiamine	10%
Cholesterol	9mg	Riboflavin	8%
Sodium	95mg	Niacin	6%
Potassium	100mg	Calcium	2%
		Iron	6%
		*Contains less than 2%	

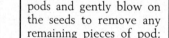

COOK'S NOTE

Cardamom

Although native to India, where it remains a popular spice, cardamom became a favorite Scandinavian seasoning for breads and pastries when early Viking traders brought it home.

About twelve of the small, hard, black seeds grow in each three-sided, creamy white, pithy pod. This pungent, aromatic spice is available as ground seeds, shelled seeds or in the pod. To remove cardamom seeds from pods, place pods in a mortar and crush with a pestle, or place pods between two sheets of waxed paper and crush them with a rolling pin or hammer. Pick out crushed pods and gently blow on the seeds to remove any remaining pieces of pod; the seeds will remain.

As with most spices, the best flavor comes from freshly crushed or ground seeds. Whole seeds can be crushed in a mortar with a pestle or ground in a pepper mill.

Julekake

BREAD
5½ to 6½ cups all purpose or
    unbleached flour
½ cup sugar
1 teaspoon salt
1 teaspoon cardamom
½ teaspoon cinnamon
2 packages active dry yeast
1 cup milk
½ cup water
⅔ cup margarine or butter
3 eggs
½ cup candied green cherries,
    halved
½ cup candied red cherries, halved
½ cup raisins

GLAZE
1½ cups powdered sugar
¼ teaspoon almond extract
2 to 3 tablespoons milk

Lightly spoon flour into measuring cup; level off. In large bowl, combine 2 cups flour, sugar, salt, cardamom, cinnamon and yeast; blend well. In small saucepan, heat 1 cup milk, water and margarine until very warm (120 to 130°F.). Add warm liquid and eggs to flour mixture. Blend at low speed until moistened; beat 3 minutes at medium speed. By hand, stir in an additional 3 to 3½ cups flour and fruit to form a soft dough. On floured surface, knead in remaining ½ to 1 cup flour until smooth

Pictured left to right: Braided Holiday Stollen; Julekake

and elastic, about 8 minutes. Place dough in greased bowl; cover loosely with plastic wrap and cloth towel. Let rise in warm place (80 to 85°F.) until light and doubled in size, about 55 to 60 minutes.

Grease 2 large cookie sheets. Punch down dough several times to remove all air bubbles. Divide dough into 3 equal parts; shape into round balls. Place on greased cookie sheets; flatten slightly. Cover; let rise in warm place until light and doubled in size, about 45 minutes.

Heat oven·to 350°F. Uncover dough. Bake at 350°F. for 30 to 35 minutes or until golden brown. Immediately re-

move from cookie sheets; cool on wire racks. In small bowl, combine all glaze ingredients, adding enough milk for desired drizzling consistency. Drizzle over cooled loaves. Garnish as desired. **3 (16-slice) loaves.**

HIGH ALTITUDE – Above 3500 Feet: No change.

NUTRITION INFORMATION PER SERVING

Serving Size: 1 slice		Percent U.S. RDA	
Calories	130	Protein	4%
Protein	2g	Vitamin A	2%
Carbohydrate	22g	Vitamin C	*
Fat	3g	Thiamine	10%
Cholesterol	14mg	Riboflavin	6%
Sodium	80mg	Niacin	4%
Potassium	50mg	Calcium	*
		Iron	4%
		*Contains less than 2%	

Julekake

This cardamom-flavored Christmas bread studded with cherries and raisins is of Scandinavian origin.

Circle of Hearts
Cherry Bread

**Circle of Hearts
Cherry Bread**

Place a red pillar candle in the center of this tea ring and use it as a centerpiece for a holiday breakfast or brunch.

FILLING
2 tablespoons cornstarch
¼ cup chopped nuts
¾ cup chopped maraschino cherries
½ cup maraschino cherry juice
1 tablespoon margarine or butter
½ teaspoon almond extract

BREAD
1 package hot roll mix
1 tablespoon sugar
1 cup water heated to 120 to 130°F.
2 tablespoons margarine or butter, softened
1 egg

GLAZE
1 cup powdered sugar
2 to 3 tablespoons milk

In small saucepan, combine all filling ingredients; cook over medium heat until mixture boils and thickens, stirring constantly. Remove from heat; set aside.

In large bowl, combine flour mixture with yeast from foil packet and sugar; blend well. Stir in *hot* water, 2 tablespoons margarine and egg until dough pulls away from sides of bowl. Turn dough out onto lightly floured surface. With greased or floured hands, shape dough into a ball. Knead dough 5 minutes until smooth. Cover with large bowl; let rest 5 minutes.

Grease cookie sheet and lightly grease outside of one 6-ounce (4-inch) custard cup. On lightly floured surface, roll dough into 18 × 12-inch rectangle. Spread warm filling over dough to within ½ inch of edges. Starting with 18-inch side, roll up tightly, pressing edges to seal. Place seam side down on greased cookie sheet. Join ends to form ring, placing greased custard cup upside down in center of ring. Pinch ends of dough to seal. With scissors or sharp knife, cut from outside edge of ring to within ½ inch of inside of ring, making 14 cuts 1¼ to 1½ inches apart. Turn 2 cut sections on their sides in opposite directions to form heart shape. Repeat to make 7 hearts. Cover loosely with plastic wrap and cloth towel. Let rise in warm place (80 to 85°F.) until light and doubled in size, about 25 to 30 minutes.

Heat oven to 375°F. Uncover dough. Bake at 375°F. for 18 to 28 minutes or until golden brown. Remove from oven; carefully remove custard cup. Remove from cookie sheet; cool on wire rack.

In small bowl, combine powdered sugar and enough milk for desired drizzling consistency. Drizzle glaze over bread, outlining hearts. Place on large serving plate. If desired, a 6-inch-tall by 3-inch-wide pillar candle can be placed in center of bread for serving.
14 servings.

HIGH ALTITUDE — Above 3500 Feet: No change.

NUTRITION INFORMATION PER SERVING

Serving Size: 1/14 of recipe		Percent U.S. RDA	
		Protein	6%
Calories	220	Vitamin A	2%
Protein	5g	Vitamin C	*
Carbohydrate	39g	Thiamine	15%
Fat	5g	Riboflavin	10%
Cholesterol	15mg	Niacin	10%
Sodium	260mg	Calcium	*
Potassium	90mg	Iron	6%
		*Contains less than 2%	

Rustic Oats and Wheat Bread

BREAD
1 cup cracked wheat
¼ cup firmly packed brown sugar
2 teaspoons salt
2 cups boiling water
¼ cup molasses
3 tablespoons oil
2 packages active dry yeast
⅔ cup water heated to 105 to 115°F.
4¾ to 5¾ cups all purpose or unbleached flour
1 cup rolled oats

TOPPING
1 egg, beaten
1 tablespoon rolled oats

In large bowl, combine cracked wheat, brown sugar, salt, 2 cups boiling water, molasses and oil; blend well. Cool mixture to 105 to 115°F.

In small bowl, dissolve yeast in ⅔ cup warm water. Add to cooled cracked wheat mixture. Lightly spoon flour into measuring cup; level off. Add 2 cups flour to cracked wheat mixture. Blend at low speed until moistened; beat 2 minutes at medium speed. By hand, stir in 1 cup rolled oats and an additional 2¼ to 2¾ cups flour until dough pulls away from sides of bowl. On floured surface, knead in remaining ½ to 1 cup flour until dough is smooth and elastic, about 10 minutes. Place dough in greased bowl; cover loosely with plastic wrap and cloth towel. Let rise in warm place (80 to 85°F.) until light and doubled in size, about 45 to 60 minutes.

Grease 2 cookie sheets. Punch dough down several times to remove all air bubbles. Divide dough in half; shape into balls. Place on greased cookie sheets. With sharp knife, slash a ¼-inch-deep lattice design in top of each loaf. Cover; let rise in warm place until light and doubled in size, about 45 to 60 minutes.

Heat oven to 350°F. Uncover dough. Brush loaves with beaten egg; sprinkle with 1 tablespoon rolled oats. Bake at 350°F. for 35 to 45 minutes or until deep golden brown and loaves sound hollow when lightly tapped. Remove from cookie sheets; cool on wire racks.
2 (16-slice) loaves.

HIGH ALTITUDE — Above 3500 Feet: Bake at 375°F. for 30 to 40 minutes.

NUTRITION INFORMATION PER SERVING

Serving Size: 1 slice		Percent U.S. RDA	
Calories	130	Protein	4%
Protein	4g	Vitamin A	*
Carbohydrate	25g	Vitamin C	*
Fat	2g	Thiamine	15%
Cholesterol	7mg	Riboflavin	8%
Sodium	140mg	Niacin	8%
Potassium	95mg	Calcium	*
		Iron	8%
*Contains less than 2%			

Cran-Apple Spiced Jelly

3½ cups sugar
1½ cups cranberry-apple drink
½ cup apple cider or juice
⅛ teaspoon cinnamon
⅛ teaspoon cloves
1 (3-ounce) package liquid fruit pectin

In large saucepan, combine sugar, cranberry-apple drink, apple cider, cinnamon and cloves. Bring to a full rolling boil, stirring to dissolve sugar. Boil 1 minute, stirring constantly. Remove from heat; stir in pectin. Skim foam. Ladle into 4 clean, hot 8-ounce jelly jars or moisture- vaporproof freezer containers, leaving ½ inch headspace. Cool slightly; cover with tight-fitting lids. Let stand several hours at room temperature or until set. Store in refrigerator up to 3 weeks or in freezer up to 3 months.
4 cups.

NUTRITION INFORMATION PER SERVING

Serving Size: 1 tablespoon		Percent U.S. RDA	
		Protein	*
Calories	45	Vitamin A	*
Protein	0g	Vitamin C	2%
Carbohydrate	12g	Thiamine	*
Fat	0g	Riboflavin	*
Cholesterol	0mg	Niacin	*
Sodium	0mg	Calcium	*
Potassium	10mg	Iron	*
*Contains less than 2%			

Rustic Oats and Wheat Bread

These large round loaves have a hearty texture and old-fashioned flavor. An electric knife works well in slicing these loaves. This bread is especially good served with soup.

Cran-Apple Spiced Jelly

This beautiful, sparkling jelly is so easy to do and can be made well ahead of the hectic holiday season. For gift-giving, select decorative jelly jars, which can be found at most supermarkets.

Cherry Twist Coffee Cake

Cherry Twist Coffee Cake

BREAD
1 package hot roll mix
3 tablespoons sugar
1 cup water heated to 120 to 130°F.
2 tablespoons margarine or butter, softened
1 egg
½ cup sugar
1 teaspoon cinnamon
½ cup chopped red candied cherries
¼ cup margarine or butter, softened

GLAZE
¾ cup powdered sugar
¼ teaspoon vanilla
3 to 5 teaspoons milk

GARNISH
Pecan halves
Candied cherries

Line 12-inch pizza pan with foil; grease foil. In large bowl, combine flour mixture with yeast from foil packet and 3 tablespoons sugar; blend well. Add *hot* water, 2 tablespoons margarine and egg; stir until dough pulls away from sides of bowl. Turn dough out onto lightly floured surface. With greased or floured hands, shape dough into a ball. Knead dough 5 minutes until smooth. Cover with large bowl; let rest 5 minutes. In small bowl, combine ½ cup sugar, cinnamon and chopped candied cherries. Set aside.

Divide dough into 3 equal parts; shape into balls. On lightly floured surface, roll out 1 ball to 12-inch circle. Place in foil-lined pan. Spread with 2 tablespoons margarine and sprinkle with ½ of cherry mixture. Roll out second ball of dough to 12-inch circle; spread with 2 tablespoons margarine. Place on top of first circle; sprinkle with remaining cherry mixture. Roll out third ball of dough to 12-inch circle; place on top.

Place 2-inch biscuit cutter in center of top circle (do not cut through dough). With sharp knife, cut through dough from cutter to outside edge, forming 16 pie-shaped wedges. Twist each wedge 5 times to form spiral pattern. Remove cutter. Cover loosely with greased plastic wrap and cloth towel. Let rise in warm place (80 to 85°F.) until light and doubled in size, about 25 to 30 minutes.

Heat oven to 375°F. Uncover dough. Bake at 375°F. for 18 to 23 minutes or until golden brown. (Place pan on foil or cookie sheet during baking to guard against spillage.) Cool slightly. Remove from pan; remove foil.

In small bowl, combine all glaze ingredients, adding enough of the milk for desired drizzling consistency; blend until smooth. Drizzle over warm coffee cake. Garnish with pecan halves and candied cherries.
16 servings.

HIGH ALTITUDE — Above 3500 Feet: No change.

NUTRITION INFORMATION PER SERVING

Serving Size: ¹⁄₁₆ of recipe		Percent U.S. RDA	
Calories	220	Protein	6%
Protein	4g	Vitamin A	4%
Carbohydrate	40g	Vitamin C	*
Fat	5g	Thiamine	10%
Cholesterol	13mg	Riboflavin	10%
Sodium	250mg	Niacin	8%
Potassium	50mg	Calcium	*
		Iron	6%
		*Contains less than 2%	

Cherry Twist Coffee Cake

This spectacular coffee cake is drizzled with glaze and topped with gleaming candied cherries. It looks complicated but it's not.

Eggnog Quick Bread

Eggnog Quick Bread

This loaf has a texture similar to pound cake and a marvelous blend of flavors for delicious eating. It's perfect for gift-giving, and we've included directions for mini-loaves. Serve plain, buttered or with Harvest Fruit Conserve.

Harvest Fruit Conserve

Conserves are a combination of several fruits and are softer than preserves or jam. This make-ahead recipe yields enough for gift-giving.

2 eggs
1 cup sugar
1 cup dairy eggnog (not canned)
½ cup margarine or butter, melted
2 teaspoons rum extract
1 teaspoon vanilla
2¼ cups all purpose or unbleached flour
2 teaspoons baking powder
½ teaspoon salt
¼ teaspoon nutmeg

Heat oven to 350°F. Grease bottom only of 9 × 5-inch loaf pan.* Beat eggs in large bowl. Add sugar, eggnog, margarine, rum extract and vanilla; blend well. Lightly spoon flour into measuring cup; level off. Add flour, baking powder, salt and nutmeg, stirring just until dry ingredients are moistened. Pour into greased pan. Bake at 350°F. for 45 to 50 minutes or until toothpick inserted in center comes out clean. Cool 10 minutes. Remove from pan. Cool completely. Wrap tightly and store in refrigerator.
1 (16-slice) loaf.

TIP: *If desired, recipe can be baked in two 5¾ × 3¼-inch loaf pans, greased on bottoms only. Bake at 350°F. for 35 to 40 minutes.

HIGH ALTITUDE—Above 3500 Feet: No change.

NUTRITION INFORMATION PER SERVING

Serving Size: 1 slice		Percent U.S. RDA	
Calories	190	Protein	4%
Protein	3g	Vitamin A	6%
Carbohydrate	28g	Vitamin C	*
Fat	8g	Thiamine	10%
Cholesterol	36mg	Riboflavin	8%
Sodium	190mg	Niacin	4%
Potassium	55mg	Calcium	4%
		Iron	4%
		*Contains less than 2%	

Harvest Fruit Conserve

½ cup chopped dried apricots
½ cup chopped dried peaches
1 cup water
1 tablespoon lemon juice
4 cups sugar
3 cups (4 medium) chopped, peeled pears
2 cups (2 medium) chopped, peeled apples

In small saucepan, combine apricots, peaches, water and lemon juice. Bring to a boil. Reduce heat; simmer uncovered 5 minutes. Set aside.

In large saucepan, combine sugar, pears and apples. Bring to a boil over medium heat, stirring constantly until sugar is melted. Reduce heat; simmer uncovered for 25 minutes, stirring occasionally. Add cooked apricot mixture. Bring to a boil; boil 5 minutes. Ladle into 5 clean, hot 8-ounce jelly jars or moisture- vaporproof freezer containers, leaving ½-inch headspace. Cool slightly; cover with tight-fitting lids. Let stand several hours at room temperature. Refrigerate at least 24 hours to thicken slightly. Store in refrigerator up to 3 weeks or in freezer up to 3 months.
5½ cups.

NUTRITION INFORMATION PER SERVING

Serving Size: 1 tablespoon		Percent U.S. RDA	
Calories	45	Protein	*
Protein	0g	Vitamin A	*
Carbohydrate	11g	Vitamin C	*
Fat	0g	Thiamine	*
Cholesterol	0mg	Riboflavin	*
Sodium	0mg	Niacin	*
Potassium	30mg	Calcium	*
		Iron	*
		*Contains less than 2%	

Apricot-Date Bread

½ cup dried apricots, cut into strips
  Boiling water
½ cup chopped dates
½ cup chopped walnuts
1 cup firmly packed brown sugar
1½ cups milk
¼ cup oil
1 egg
2¾ cups all purpose or unbleached
  flour
¾ teaspoon baking powder
¾ teaspoon baking soda
¾ teaspoon salt

Heat oven to 350°F. Grease and flour bottom only of 9 × 5-inch loaf pan. In small bowl, cover apricots with boiling water and let stand 5 minutes. Drain; add dates and walnuts. In large bowl, combine brown sugar, milk, oil and egg; mix well. Lightly spoon flour into measuring cup; level off. Add flour, baking powder, baking soda and salt to brown sugar mixture, stirring just until moistened. Stir in apricot mixture. Pour into greased and floured pan.

Bake at 350°F. for 60 to 70 minutes or until toothpick inserted in center comes out clean. Cool 10 minutes; remove from pan. Cool completely. Wrap tightly and store in refrigerator.
1 (16-slice) loaf.

HIGH ALTITUDE – Above 3500 Feet: No change.

NUTRITION INFORMATION PER SERVING

Serving Size: 1 slice		Percent U.S. RDA	
Calories	220	Protein	6%
Protein	4g	Vitamin A	6%
Carbohydrate	38g	Vitamin C	*
Fat	7g	Thiamine	10%
Cholesterol	15mg	Riboflavin	10%
Sodium	190mg	Niacin	8%
Potassium	220mg	Calcium	6%
		Iron	10%
*Contains less than 2%			

Orange-Cream Cheese Spread

1 (8-ounce) package cream cheese,
  softened
¼ cup orange marmalade

In small bowl, beat cream cheese until light and fluffy. Gradually add orange marmalade, beating until well combined. Store in refrigerator.
1 cup.

NUTRITION INFORMATION PER SERVING

Serving Size: 1 tablespoon		Percent U.S. RDA	
Calories	60	Protein	*
Protein	1g	Vitamin A	4%
Carbohydrate	4g	Vitamin C	*
Fat	5g	Thiamine	*
Cholesterol	16mg	Riboflavin	*
Sodium	45mg	Niacin	*
Potassium	20mg	Calcium	*
		Iron	*
*Contains less than 2%			

Apricot-Date Bread

Combined with a container of Orange-Cream Cheese Spread, this bread would make a great gift for a teacher or Scout leader.

COOK'S NOTE

Loaves

Well-wrapped loaves of cooled quick breads can be stored up to a week in the refrigerator. Or wrap, label and freeze them for up to three months. Remember, a lengthwise crack on the top crust of quick breads is characteristic. Loaves should be thoroughly cooled before slicing them with a sharp bread knife. Flavors and slicing often improve the day after baking.

Grand Finales

Desserts That Add the Finishing Touch to Holiday Meals

The lights have dimmed, the candles burned down. The dishes are cleared and belts have been loosened. The aroma of fresh coffee wafts from the kitchen. But this lull in the Christmas festivities soon yields to the grand finale — dessert, the crowning glory to any holiday meal.

And oh, what desserts — from easy to elaborate, traditional to contemporary, desserts that make the most of winter fruits, that add a flavor twist to old favorites. In this collection, there's just the right dessert to fit your entertaining occasion whether it's an elegant dinner party for neighbors, an after-caroling buffet, Christmas Eve gift opening, or a thank-you party for co-workers like the one held each year by our Pillsbury staff.

Guests gather on a snowy evening just before Christmas for a "white elephant" gift exchange. They bring intriguingly wrapped treasures unearthed from their attics and garages. The givers remain anonymous and the hostess distributes the gifts — some of which crop up year after year. Following the laughter and groans, a selection of festive desserts is served. It's an inexpensive and delicious alternative to a formal dinner.

But if formal dinners figure into your holiday entertaining, you'll find an array of elegant yet simple-to-prepare desserts: Chocolate Glazed Russe de Strawberry encircled with flame-red ribbon, Cran-Raspberry Sorbet for a light finish to a meal. Or serve a Warm Cranberry Alexander, a beverage that thinks it's a dessert, with an assortment of holiday cookies.

Desserts may be delectable, but they also can be the centerpiece of family traditions. Mrs. Cratchit thrilled Tiny Tim with a flaming pudding studded with plums and nuts. And now you can create your own steamed Christmas pudding, Cranberry Pudding with Butter Sauce — *in the microwave!*

You'll win over new and old fruitcake fans with one of three variations: Festive Fruitcake dotted with candied fruits, Applesauce Fruitcake laden with dates, raisins and nuts, or Festive Chocolate Fruitcake sprinkled with chocolate chips and candied pineapple.

Snowy Christmas Cake

Gift Suggestions

For Dessert Enthusiasts

Springform pan
Assortment of cake
  pans — round, square,
  rectangular, tube or
  fluted tube
Serving plates — crystal,
  china, silver or con-
  temporary
Covered carriers for
  cakes or pies
Assortment of coffees or
  teas
Unique dessert service
  for two or more
Pie server
Cake server or knife
Demitasse set
Decanter with cordial
  glasses
Decorator/pastry tubes

CAKE
  2 (8-inch) round baked cake layers
  (use favorite cake mix or recipe)

TREES
  2 ounces (2 squares) semi-sweet
  chocolate
  2 teaspoons shortening

FROSTING
  2 egg whites
  ¼ teaspoon salt
  1½ teaspoons vanilla
  ¼ cup sugar
  ¾ cup light corn syrup
  ⅓ cup coconut

Using a pastry brush or hand, brush loose crumbs from sides of each cake layer. If desired, to keep serving plate clean arrange strips of waxed paper around edge of plate. Place 1 cake layer, top side down, on serving plate.

To prepare trees, trace tree pattern on white paper. Cut eight 4 × 3½-inch pieces of waxed paper; set aside. In small saucepan over medium heat, melt chocolate and shortening, stirring constantly. Cool slightly. Pour chocolate mixture into small squeeze bottle or plastic bag with writing tip. (A number 3 writing tip works well.) Place pattern piece on cookie sheet. Lay 1 piece of waxed paper over pattern. Pipe chocolate over outline, making ¼-inch-wide lines. Carefully slip out pattern. Repeat to make 8 trees. Refrigerate 30 minutes or until ready to use.

To prepare frosting, in small deep bowl beat egg whites, salt and vanilla at medium speed until foamy. Gradually add sugar 1 tablespoon at a time, beating at high speed until soft peaks form and sugar is dissolved. In small saucepan over medium heat, bring corn syrup just to a boil. Pour in thin stream over egg whites while beating at high speed until mixture is stiff.

Spread about ¼ of frosting evenly over first layer. Place remaining layer, top side up, on frosted layer. Spread sides of cake with a very thin coat of frosting to seal in crumbs. Using about ⅔ of remaining frosting, frost sides of cake with upward strokes, bringing frosting up high on sides of cake. Spread remaining frosting over top of cake just to edge of frosted sides. Make decorative swirls or leave smooth. Sprinkle top with coconut. Carefully remove waxed paper strips from around bottom edge of cake. Carefully remove chocolate trees from waxed paper. Space evenly around sides of cake.
12 servings.

NUTRITION INFORMATION PER SERVING

Serving Size: 1/12 of recipe using white cake mix		Percent U.S. RDA	
		Protein	4%
		Vitamin A	*
Calories	330	Vitamin C	*
Protein	3g	Thiamine	4%
Carbohydrate	53g	Riboflavin	6%
Fat	12g	Niacin	4%
Cholesterol	2mg	Calcium	4%
Sodium	240mg	Iron	8%
Potassium	75mg	*Contains less than 2%	

Pattern for Chocolate Tree

Pictured on preceding pages:
Snowy Christmas Cake

Festive Pear Tart

Festive Pear Tart

1 (29-ounce) can pear halves,
    drained
4 cups cranberry juice cocktail
1 (15-ounce) package refrigerated
    pie crusts
⅓ cup sugar
1 (8-ounce) package cream cheese,
    softened
1 teaspoon almond extract
    Seedless green grapes
¼ cup apple jelly

Arrange pears, rounded side down, in single layer in 12 × 8-inch (2-quart) baking dish. Pour cranberry juice over pears to cover completely. Cover; refrigerate overnight.

Heat oven to 450°F. Prepare pie crust according to package directions for *unfilled one-crust pie*, using 10-inch tart pan with removable bottom or 9-inch pie pan; trim edges if necessary. (Refrigerate remaining crust for a later use.) Bake at 450°F. for 9 to 11 minutes or until light golden brown. Cool completely.

In medium bowl, combine sugar, cream cheese and almond extract; blend well. Spread evenly in cooled crust. Drain pears.* Thinly slice pears lengthwise, keeping slices together. Fan out slices and arrange over filling. Place grapes between pears to fill spaces. Heat apple jelly in small saucepan until melted; brush over fruit. Store in refrigerator. **8 servings.**

TIP: *Drained cranberry juice can be used as desired.

NUTRITION INFORMATION PER SERVING

Serving Size: ⅛ of recipe		Percent U.S. RDA	
		Protein	4%
Calories	320	Vitamin A	8%
Protein	3g	Vitamin C	6%
Carbohydrate	39g	Thiamine	*
Fat	17g	Riboflavin	4%
Cholesterol	38mg	Niacin	*
Sodium	190mg	Calcium	2%
Potassium	125mg	Iron	4%
		*Contains less than 2%	

Festive Pear Tart

This elegant tart features crimson pear slices fanned over an easy, creamy filling. Pears soak overnight in cranberry juice to become a beautiful crimson.

Chocolate Glazed Russe de Strawberry

Chocolate Glazed Russe de Strawberry

Chocolate Glazed Russe de Strawberry

A red satin ribbon sets off this dessert, which is especially impressive when served on a pedestal plate. Garnish it with fresh strawberries or purchased marzipan strawberries.

CRUST
18 ladyfingers, halved lengthwise
¼ cup orange-flavored liqueur

FILLING
2 envelopes unflavored gelatin
¾ cup cold water
1 pint (2 cups) fresh strawberries, hulls removed, or 2 cups frozen strawberries without syrup, thawed
½ to ¾ cup sugar
3 tablespoons lemon juice
1 pint (2 cups) whipping cream

GLAZE
2 ounces (2 squares) semi-sweet chocolate, cut into pieces
2 tablespoons margarine or butter

GARNISH
1⅜ yards (½-inch) red satin ribbon
10 whole fresh strawberries

Butter bottom only of 9-inch spring-form pan. Sprinkle cut side of ladyfingers with liqueur. Place ladyfingers, cut sides facing in, around sides and in bottom of buttered pan.

In small saucepan, soften gelatin in cold water; stir over low heat until dissolved. Remove from heat. In large bowl, mash strawberries; by hand, beat in sugar, lemon juice and dissolved gelatin until foamy. Refrigerate just until mixture thickens slightly, about 20 minutes.*

In small bowl, beat whipping cream until stiff peaks form; fold into strawberry mixture. Pour into ladyfinger-lined pan. Refrigerate at least 4 hours.

Line cookie sheet with waxed paper. Draw a 6½-inch circle on paper. In small saucepan over low heat, melt chocolate and margarine. Spread chocolate mixture evenly over 6½-inch circle on waxed paper-lined cookie sheet. Refrigerate until slightly hardened, 40 to 50 minutes. Cut circle into 10 equal wedges. Gently lift wedges from waxed paper; arrange over strawberry mixture. Carefully remove sides of pan. Tie ribbon around dessert. Garnish with strawberries.

10 servings.

MICROWAVE DIRECTIONS: Prepare pan and ladyfingers as directed above. In 2-cup microwave-safe measuring cup, combine gelatin and cold water. Let stand 5 minutes. Microwave on HIGH for 30 to 45 seconds or until gelatin is dissolved. *Do not boil.* Continue as directed above. To prepare glaze, in 1-cup microwave-safe measuring cup combine chocolate and margarine. Microwave on MEDIUM for 1½ to 2 minutes, stirring once halfway through cooking. Stir until smooth. Continue as directed above.

TIP: *When using frozen strawberries, refrigerate mixture about 5 minutes.

NUTRITION INFORMATION PER SERVING

Serving Size: ¹⁄₁₀ of recipe		Percent U.S. RDA	
		Protein	6%
Calories	380	Vitamin A	20%
Protein	4g	Vitamin C	50%
Carbohydrate	41g	Thiamine	4%
Fat	24g	Riboflavin	8%
Cholesterol	136mg	Niacin	2%
Sodium	60mg	Calcium	4%
Potassium	160mg	Iron	4%

Norwegian Hazelnut Cake

CAKE
- 2 (2½-ounce) packages hazelnuts (filberts) or pecans
- ½ cup butter or margarine
- 3 eggs
- 1½ cups sugar
- 1 teaspoon vanilla
- 2 cups all purpose or unbleached flour
- 2 teaspoons baking powder
- ¼ teaspoon salt

GLAZE
- ½ cup whipping cream
- 1 (6-ounce) package (1 cup) semi-sweet chocolate chips
- ½ teaspoon vanilla

Heat oven to 350°F. Lightly grease bottom only of 10-inch springform pan.* Reserve 8 whole nuts for garnish. In food processor bowl with metal blade or blender container, process nuts until ground (about 1⅓ cups); reserve 1 tablespoon for garnish.

Melt butter in small saucepan over low heat; cool. In large bowl, beat eggs, sugar and 1 teaspoon vanilla until thick and lemon-colored, 2 to 3 minutes. Lightly spoon flour into measuring cup; level off. Add flour, baking powder, salt and ground nuts; mix well. Continue beating, gradually adding cooled melted butter until well blended. (Mixture will be thick.) Spread batter in greased pan.

Bake at 350°F. for 35 to 45 minutes or until toothpick inserted in center comes out clean. Cool 15 minutes; remove sides of pan. Run long knife under cake to loosen from pan bottom; invert onto serving plate. Cover with cloth towel; cool about 30 minutes.

To prepare glaze, in medium saucepan bring whipping cream just to a boil; remove from heat. Stir in chocolate chips until melted and smooth; add ½ teaspoon vanilla. Spread glaze over top of cake, allowing some to run down sides. Sprinkle reserved ground nuts around top edge of cake; arrange reserved whole nuts over ground nuts.

16 servings.

TIP: *A 9-inch round cake pan can be substituted. Line pan with foil; grease well. Continue as directed above. Bake at 350°F. for 45 to 55 minutes.

HIGH ALTITUDE—Above 3500 Feet: Increase flour to 2 cups plus 2 tablespoons. Bake at 375°F. for 30 to 40 minutes.

NUTRITION INFORMATION PER SERVING

Serving Size: ¹⁄₁₆ of recipe		Percent U.S. RDA	
		Protein	6%
Calories	330	Vitamin A	8%
Protein	5g	Vitamin C	*
Carbohydrate	38g	Thiamine	10%
Fat	19g	Riboflavin	8%
Cholesterol	66mg	Niacin	4%
Sodium	140mg	Calcium	6%
Potassium	110mg	Iron	8%
		*Contains less than 2%	

Norwegian Hazelnut Cake

When the occasion calls for something special, serve this fabulous nut-filled cake.

COOK'S NOTE

Storing Cakes

Frosted or unfrosted cakes left in the baking pan are easily stored by covering the pan with its own lid or with a tight covering of foil or plastic wrap. Frosted layer and tube cakes retain their moistness and attractive appearance when stored under a cake cover or similar device that keeps out drying air without touching the frosting.

Yule Log Cake; Meringue Mushrooms, page 16

Yule Log Cake

Powdered sugar

CAKE
- ½ cup all purpose or unbleached flour
- ¼ cup unsweetened cocoa
- 1 teaspoon baking powder
- ¼ teaspoon salt
- 4 eggs, separated
- ¾ cup sugar
- 1 teaspoon vanilla
- 2 tablespoons water

FILLING AND FROSTING
- 1 can ready-to-spread coconut pecan frosting
- 1 can ready-to-spread chocolate fudge frosting

GARNISH
- Meringue Mushrooms (see page 16)

Heat oven to 350°F. Generously grease bottom only of 15 × 10 × 1-inch baking pan; line with waxed paper and grease again. Lightly sprinkle clean towel with powdered sugar. Lightly spoon flour into measuring cup; level off. In small bowl, combine flour, cocoa, baking powder and salt; set aside. In small bowl, beat egg whites until foamy. Gradually add half of sugar, beating continuously until stiff peaks form. Set aside.

In large bowl, beat egg yolks until thick. Add remaining sugar and vanilla; beat until very thick. Stir in water. Gradually fold flour mixture into egg yolk mixture. Gently fold in beaten egg whites. Spread batter in greased and waxed paper-lined pan. Bake at 350°F. for 18 to 22 minutes or until toothpick inserted in center comes out clean. Loosen edges; immediately invert cake onto powdered-sugar towel. Remove waxed paper. Starting at shorter end, roll up cake in towel; cool completely on wire rack.

Unroll cooled cake; remove towel. Spread cake with coconut pecan frosting; roll up again, rolling loosely to incorporate filling. Place on serving plate. Frost sides and top of filled cake roll with chocolate fudge frosting. With fork, comb frosting to resemble bark. Garnish with Meringue Mushrooms.
10 servings.

HIGH ALTITUDE—Above 3500 Feet: Decrease baking powder to ½ teaspoon. Bake at 375°F. for 12 to 15 minutes.

NUTRITION INFORMATION PER SERVING

Serving Size: ¹⁄₁₀ of recipe		Percent U.S. RDA	
		Protein	6%
Calories	490	Vitamin A	2%
Protein	5g	Vitamin C	*
Carbohydrate	71g	Thiamine	6%
Fat	22g	Riboflavin	8%
Cholesterol	85mg	Niacin	2%
Sodium	300mg	Calcium	4%
Potassium	240mg	Iron	10%
		*Contains less than 2%	

Yule Log Cake

Canned frostings simplify the filling and frosting of this dessert, also known as Bûche de Noël. It was originally inspired by the French custom of burning a Christmas log of such great size that, once lighted, it would last through Christmas Eve supper.

COOK'S NOTE

Dessert Plate Brighteners

Brighten a dessert party for adults with soft candle glow by using the small candle holders designed to clip candles onto Christmas tree branches. Insert a candle, clip one to each dessert plate and light the candles just before serving for a sparkling, festive touch.

Applesauce Fruitcake

Applesauce Fruitcake

This fruitcake doesn't require the long aging usually needed for the traditional version. And it's perfect for those who don't care for the citron in most fruitcakes.

Festive Chocolate Fruitcake

You'll love the convenience of this "Christmas cake" made from a mix. Full of fruits and nuts and rich chocolate flavor, it slices beautifully right from the refrigerator.

1½ cups sugar
1 cup shortening
2 eggs
3¼ cups all purpose or unbleached flour
1½ teaspoons baking soda
2 teaspoons cinnamon
1 teaspoon allspice
1 teaspoon cloves
½ teaspoon salt
1½ cups chopped nuts
1½ cups raisins
1½ cups coarsely chopped dates
½ cup coarsely chopped red maraschino cherries, drained*
2 cups applesauce
6 red maraschino cherries, halved
6 pecan halves

Heat oven to 325°F. Grease 10-inch tube pan; line bottom with waxed paper or foil and grease again. In large bowl, beat sugar and shortening until light and fluffy. Add eggs; blend well. Lightly spoon flour into measuring cup; level off. Reserve ½ cup flour. Add remaining 2¾ cups flour, baking soda, cinnamon, allspice, cloves and salt to egg mixture. Blend at low speed until moistened; beat 2 minutes at medium speed.

In large bowl, combine ½ cup reserved flour with nuts, raisins, dates and ½ cup cherries; stir until nuts and fruit are lightly coated. By hand, stir nut-fruit mixture and applesauce into batter; mix well. Pour batter into greased and waxed paper-lined pan; top with cherry halves and pecans.

Bake at 325°F. for 1¼ to 1¾ hours or until toothpick inserted in center comes out clean. Cool upright in pan 5 minutes. Remove from pan; remove waxed paper. Turn upright onto wire rack; cool completely. Wrap cooled cake in plastic wrap or foil to keep moist. Store in refrigerator.
20 servings.

TIP: *Candied cherries can be substituted for maraschino cherries.

HIGH ALTITUDE—Above 3500 Feet: No change.

NUTRITION INFORMATION PER SERVING

Serving Size: ½₀ of recipe		Percent U.S. RDA	
		Protein	6%
Calories	380	Vitamin A	*
Protein	5g	Vitamin C	*
Carbohydrate	58g	Thiamine	15%
Fat	17g	Riboflavin	10%
Cholesterol	21mg	Niacin	8%
Sodium	150mg	Calcium	2%
Potassium	260mg	Iron	10%

*Contains less than 2%

Festive Chocolate Fruitcake

1 package pudding-included devil's food cake mix
⅓ cup whiskey or water
1 (8-ounce) carton dairy sour cream
3 eggs
2 cups chopped pecans
1 cup golden raisins
1 cup halved red maraschino cherries, drained
1 (8-ounce) container candied pineapple pieces, halved
1 (6-ounce) package (1 cup) semi-sweet chocolate chips
Corn syrup, if desired

Heat oven to 350°F. Grease and flour 12-cup fluted tube pan. In large bowl, combine cake mix, whiskey, sour cream and eggs at low speed until moistened; beat 2 minutes at high speed. Stir in remaining ingredients except corn syrup. Pour into greased and floured pan.

Bake at 350°F. for 50 to 60 minutes or until cake springs back when touched lightly in center. Cool 20 minutes. Remove from pan; cool completely. Wrap tightly and refrigerate overnight.

Brush with warm corn syrup before serving. Decorate with additional candied fruits and nuts, if desired. Slice thin to serve. Store in refrigerator for up to 2 weeks.
24 servings.

HIGH ALTITUDE—Above 3500 Feet: Add ¼ cup flour to dry cake mix. Bake as directed above.

NUTRITION INFORMATION PER SERVING

Serving Size: ½₄ of recipe		Percent U.S. RDA	
		Protein	4%
Calories	280	Vitamin A	2%
Protein	4g	Vitamin C	10%
Carbohydrate	39g	Thiamine	8%
Fat	14g	Riboflavin	6%
Cholesterol	31mg	Niacin	4%
Sodium	170mg	Calcium	8%
Potassium	300mg	Iron	6%

Festive Fruitcake

Festive Fruitcake

2 cups water
2 tablespoons oil
2 eggs
2 packages date or nut bread mix
2 cups pecan halves or chopped pecans
2 cups raisins
2 cups (12 to 13 ounces) candied cherries
1 cup cut-up candied pineapple
Corn syrup, if desired

Heat oven to 350°F. Grease and flour bottom and sides of 12-cup fluted tube pan or 10-inch tube pan.* In large bowl, combine water, oil and eggs. Add remaining ingredients except corn syrup; stir by hand until combined. Pour into greased and floured pan. Bake at 350°F. for 75 to 85 minutes or until toothpick inserted in center comes out clean. Cool in pan 30 minutes. Loosen edges and remove from pan. Cool completely. Wrap tightly and refrigerate overnight.

Brush with warm corn syrup before serving. Decorate with additional candied fruits and nuts, if desired. Slice thin to serve. Store in refrigerator for up to 2 weeks or freezer for up to 3 months.
24 to 36 servings.

TIP: *If desired, recipe can be baked in the following pans:

Two (8×4 or 9×5-inch) loaf pans: Grease bottom and sides of pans. Bake 65 to 75 minutes. 2 loaves.

Muffin cups: Line cups with paper baking cups; fill ⅔ full. Bake 20 to 25 minutes. About 3½ dozen.

HIGH ALTITUDE — Above 3500 Feet: Add ¼ cup flour to dry bread mix. For 12-cup fluted tube pan or 10-inch tube pan, bake at 350°F. for 80 to 90 minutes.

NUTRITION INFORMATION PER SERVING

Serving Size: ¹⁄₃₆ of recipe		Percent U.S. RDA	
Calories	220	Protein	4%
		Vitamin A	*
Protein	2g	Vitamin C	4%
Carbohydrate	42g	Thiamine	8%
Fat	6g	Riboflavin	4%
Cholesterol	12mg	Niacin	4%
Sodium	100mg	Calcium	2%
Potassium	170mg	Iron	4%
		*Contains less than 2%	

Festive Fruitcake

An easy-to-make version of the traditional fruitcake. Note the shaping options in the Tip.

Chocolate Mousse de Menthe

This lucious, creamy dessert is ready to serve in minutes! Serve it in stemmed goblets or special dessert dishes and garnish it with Marbled Chocolate Curls.

Frozen Pistachio Cream Dessert with Ruby Raspberry Sauce

The exceptional appearance and flavor of this frozen dessert makes it perfect for holiday entertaining. For easier serving, place the frozen dessert in the refrigerator about 1 hour before serving to soften it.

Chocolate Mousse de Menthe

1 (3-ounce) package cream cheese
¼ cup semi-sweet chocolate chips
1 tablespoon white crème de menthe liqueur or ¼ teaspoon mint extract
1 cup whipping cream
¼ cup powdered sugar
Marbled Chocolate Curls, if desired

MICROWAVE DIRECTIONS: In 2-cup microwave-safe measuring cup, combine cream cheese and chocolate chips. Microwave on HIGH for 30 to 40 seconds or until cream cheese and chocolate are softened; stir to blend. Add liqueur; mix well.

In small bowl, beat whipping cream until soft peaks form. Blend in powdered sugar; beat until stiff peaks form. Fold in chocolate mixture. Spoon into individual dessert dishes. Garnish with Marbled Chocolate Curls. Serve immediately.

4 (½-cup) servings.

NUTRITION INFORMATION PER SERVING

Serving Size: ½ cup		Percent U.S. RDA	
Calories	410	Protein	6%
Protein	4g	Vitamin A	25%
Carbohydrate	20g	Vitamin C	*
Fat	36g	Thiamine	*
Cholesterol	106mg	Riboflavin	6%
Sodium	90mg	Niacin	*
Potassium	125mg	Calcium	6%
		Iron	2%
		*Contains less than 2%	

Marbled Chocolate Curls

Place 1 ounce (1 square) semi-sweet chocolate in small microwave-safe bowl. Microwave on MEDIUM for 2 to 2½ minutes or until chocolate is melted. Stir until smooth. In another small microwave-safe bowl, place 1 ounce vanilla-flavored candy coating. Microwave on MEDIUM for 1½ to 2 minutes or until vanilla coating is melted. Stir until smooth. With spatula, spread melted chocolate and vanilla coating in thin marbled layer on inverted cookie sheet. Refrigerate just until firm but not brittle, about 10 minutes. Using metal spatula or pancake turner, scrape chocolate from pan, making curls. (Chocolate curls will be as wide as the spatula. For small curls use narrow spatula; for larger curls use pancake turner.) Use toothpick to transfer curls to dessert.

Frozen Pistachio Cream Dessert with Ruby Raspberry Sauce

CRUST
1 cup (about 27) crushed vanilla wafers
½ cup finely chopped red pistachios
¼ cup margarine or butter, melted

FILLING
2 (3-ounce) packages cream cheese, softened
1 (3½-ounce) package instant pistachio pudding and pie filling mix
1¼ cups milk
1 (8-ounce) container frozen whipped topping, thawed

RUBY RASPBERRY SAUCE
1 (10-ounce) package frozen raspberries, partially thawed
2 tablespoons sugar
2 tablespoons orange-flavored liqueur

GARNISH
Reserved ¾ cup whipped topping
2 tablespoons chopped red pistachios

In medium bowl, combine all crust ingredients; blend well. Press firmly in bottom of ungreased 8-inch springform or 8-inch square pan.

In small bowl, beat cream cheese until light and fluffy. Add pudding mix and milk; beat until smooth. Reserve ¾ cup of the whipped topping; cover and refrigerate. Fold remaining whipped top-

Frozen Pistachio Cream Dessert with Ruby Raspberry Sauce

ping into cream cheese mixture; spoon into crust-lined pan. Freeze 5 hours or overnight until firm.

In blender container or food processor bowl with metal blade, combine raspberries, sugar and liqueur. Cover; blend until smooth. Strain to remove seeds. Before serving, let dessert thaw in refrigerator about 1 hour.

Top with reserved whipped topping, Ruby Raspberry Sauce and 2 tablespoons chopped pistachios.

9 servings.

NUTRITION INFORMATION PER SERVING

Serving Size: ⅑ of recipe		Percent U.S. RDA	
		Protein	8%
Calories	410	Vitamin A	15%
Protein	5g	Vitamin C	10%
Carbohydrate	43g	Thiamine	6%
Fat	25g	Riboflavin	8%
Cholesterol	28mg	Niacin	2%
Sodium	210mg	Calcium	10%
Potassium	220mg	Iron	6%

Frozen Cranberry Pie

1 (15-ounce) package refrigerated pie crusts

FILLING
2 cups fresh or frozen cranberries, coarsely chopped
1 cup sugar
1 tablespoon frozen orange juice concentrate
1 teaspoon vanilla
⅛ teaspoon salt
1½ cups whipping cream

GLAZE
¼ cup sugar
1 tablespoon cornstarch
½ cup fresh or frozen cranberries
⅓ cup water

Heat oven to 450°F. Prepare pie crust according to package directions for *unfilled one-crust pie* using 9-inch pie pan. (Refrigerate remaining crust for a later use.) Bake at 450°F. for 9 to 11 minutes or until light golden brown. Cool completely.

In large bowl, combine 2 cups cranberries and 1 cup sugar; let stand 5 to 10 minutes or until sugar is dissolved. Stir in orange juice concentrate, vanilla and salt until blended. In small bowl, beat whipping cream until soft peaks form; fold into cranberry mixture. Pour into cooled crust. Freeze until firm.

In small saucepan, combine ¼ cup sugar and cornstarch; add ½ cup cranberries and water. Cook until mixture boils and thickens, stirring constantly. Cool completely. Just before serving, spoon glaze onto top of pie and spread it into a star shape.
8 servings.

NUTRITION INFORMATION PER SERVING

Serving Size: ⅛ of recipe		Percent U.S. RDA	
		Protein	2%
Calories	410	Vitamin A	15%
Protein	2g	Vitamin C	10%
Carbohydrate	50g	Thiamine	*
Fat	24g	Riboflavin	2%
Cholesterol	68mg	Niacin	*
Sodium	160mg	Calcium	2%
Potassium	85mg	Iron	*
		*Contains less than 2%	

Frozen Cranberry Pie

Make and freeze this fluffy pink pie ahead of time, then top it with a cranberry glaze star just before serving it.

COOK'S NOTE

Easy Pie Crust Edge Cover

To prevent excessive browning of the fluted edge of a pie crust, follow these steps to make foil into an edge cover:
• Using 12-inch-wide foil, cut a piece 4 inches longer than the diameter of the pie pan.
• Cut a circle out of the center of the foil that is 2 inches smaller than the diameter of the pie pan.
• After 15 to 20 minutes of baking, center foil over pie. Gently fold foil over fluted edge. Continue baking.

Maple Pecan Pumpkin Pie

1 (15-ounce) package refrigerated pie crusts

FILLING
½ cup sugar
1 teaspoon cinnamon
½ teaspoon salt
¼ cup raisins
¼ cup chopped pecans
1 (16-ounce) can (2 cups) pumpkin
1 (12-ounce) can (1½ cups) evaporated milk
1 teaspoon maple extract
2 eggs, slightly beaten

TOPPING
1½ cups whipping cream
¼ cup powdered sugar
½ teaspoon maple extract
Pecan halves

Prepare pie crust according to package directions for *filled one-crust pie.* (Refrigerate remaining pie crust for a later use.) Heat oven to 425°F.

In large bowl, combine all filling ingredients; blend well. Pour into pie crust-lined pan. Bake at 425°F. for 15 minutes. Reduce oven temperature to 350°F.; bake an additional 40 to 45 minutes or until knife inserted near center comes out clean. Cool completely.

In small bowl, whip cream until soft peaks form. Add powdered sugar and maple extract; whip until firm peaks form. Spread over cooled pie. Refrigerate until ready to serve. Garnish with pecans, if desired.
8 to 10 servings.

NUTRITION INFORMATION PER SERVING

Serving Size: 1/10 of recipe		Percent U.S. RDA	
		Protein	10%
Calories	400	Vitamin A	220%
Protein	6g	Vitamin C	2%
Carbohydrate	45g	Thiamine	4%
Fat	23g	Riboflavin	15%
Cholesterol	98mg	Niacin	*
Sodium	260mg	Calcium	15%
Potassium	310mg	Iron	6%
		*Contains less than 2%	

Old-Fashioned Gingerbread with Lemon Sauce

⅓ cup margarine or butter, softened
½ cup sugar
1 cup dark molasses
3 eggs
3 cups all purpose or unbleached flour
1½ teaspoons baking soda
½ teaspoon salt
1½ teaspoons ginger
1½ teaspoons cinnamon
¾ teaspoon nutmeg
¾ teaspoon allspice
½ teaspoon cloves
¾ cup buttermilk*

LEMON SAUCE
½ cup sugar
1 tablespoon cornstarch
⅛ teaspoon salt
1 cup boiling water
2 tablespoons margarine or butter
1 teaspoon grated lemon peel
3 tablespoons lemon juice

Heat oven to 350°F. Grease and flour bottoms only of two 8 × 4 or 9 × 5-inch loaf pans. In large bowl, combine ⅓ cup margarine and ½ cup sugar; beat until light and fluffy. Add molasses and eggs; blend well. Lightly spoon flour into measuring cup; level off. In medium bowl, combine flour, baking soda, ½ teaspoon salt, ginger, cinnamon, nutmeg, allspice and cloves; mix well. Add dry ingredients to molasses mixture alternately with buttermilk, beating well after each addition. Pour into greased and floured pans. Bake at 350°F. for 45 to 55 minutes or until toothpick inserted in center comes out clean. Cool 15 minutes. Remove from pans; cool on wire racks.

In medium saucepan, combine ½ cup sugar, cornstarch and ⅛ teaspoon salt; mix well. Gradually stir in boiling water. Bring to a boil; cook over medium heat for 5 minutes or until thickened, stirring constantly. Remove from heat. Add 2 tablespoons margarine, lemon peel and lemon juice; mix well. Carefully cut gingerbread into 1-inch slices. Serve warm lemon sauce over gingerbread.

12 to 16 servings.

TIP: *To substitute for buttermilk, use 2 teaspoons vinegar or lemon juice plus milk to make ¾ cup.

HIGH ALTITUDE — Above 3500 Feet: Bake at 375°F. for 35 to 45 minutes.

NUTRITION INFORMATION PER SERVING

Serving Size: 1⁄16 of recipe		Percent U.S. RDA	
Calories	250	Protein	6%
Protein	4g	Vitamin A	6%
Carbohydrate	44g	Vitamin C	*
Fat	7g	Thiamine	15%
Cholesterol	40mg	Riboflavin	10%
Sodium	280mg	Niacin	8%
Potassium	280mg	Calcium	8%
		Iron	15%
		*Contains less than 2%	

Cran-Raspberry Sorbet

1 (3-ounce) package black-raspberry-flavor gelatin
½ cup boiling water
1½ cups cranberry juice cocktail

In large bowl, dissolve gelatin in boiling water. Stir in cranberry juice. Freeze until mixture is partially frozen. Beat until fluffy, about 2 minutes. Pour into freezer container; cover. Freeze until firm.

6 (½-cup) servings.

NUTRITION INFORMATION PER SERVING

Serving Size: ½ cup		Percent U.S. RDA	
Calories	90	Protein	2%
Protein	1g	Vitamin A	*
Carbohydrate	22g	Vitamin C	35%
Fat	0g	Thiamine	*
Cholesterol	0mg	Riboflavin	*
Sodium	45mg	Niacin	*
Potassium	40mg	Calcium	*
		Iron	*
		*Contains less than 2%	

Cran-Raspberry Sorbet

Divine desserts don't have to be calorie-laden. Serve this after a heavy meal or as a brunch dessert.

COOK'S NOTE

Sorbet

A French dessert containing no milk or eggs and featuring fruit, fruit juices, sweeteners and sometimes liqueurs. It must be stirred during freezing and should be eaten soon after freezing.

Cranberry Pudding with Butter Sauce

Cranberry Pudding with Butter Sauce

1½ cups dry white bread crumbs
1 cup sugar
1 tablespoon flour
1½ teaspoons baking powder
¼ teaspoon salt
¼ teaspoon ginger
¼ teaspoon cinnamon
⅛ to ¼ teaspoon allspice
⅓ cup butter or margarine, melted
⅓ cup milk
1 cup coarsely chopped fresh or frozen cranberries (do not thaw)
1 egg, slightly beaten

BUTTER SAUCE
½ cup sugar
1 teaspoon cornstarch
½ cup whipping cream
¼ cup butter or margarine, melted
½ teaspoon vanilla

MICROWAVE DIRECTIONS: Grease bottom only of 4-cup microwave-safe measuring cup; line bottom with waxed paper and grease again. In large bowl, combine bread crumbs, 1 cup sugar, flour, baking powder, salt, ginger, cinnamon and allspice. Add ⅓ cup butter, milk, cranberries and egg; mix well. (Mixture will be stiff.) Spoon batter into greased and waxed paper-lined measuring cup; press down slightly. Cover tightly with microwave-safe plastic wrap. Microwave on MEDIUM for 11 to 14 minutes, rotating measuring cup ½ turn halfway through cooking. Pudding is done when it starts to pull away from sides of measuring cup. Uncover; let container stand on flat surface 5 minutes. Loosen pudding from sides of measuring cup; invert onto serving plate. Remove waxed paper. Cool.

In 4-cup microwave-safe measuring cup, combine ½ cup sugar and cornstarch. Stir in whipping cream and ¼ cup butter. Microwave on HIGH for 1½ to 2 minutes or until mixture boils, stirring once during cooking. Microwave on HIGH for 1 minute. Stir in vanilla. Cut pudding into wedges. Serve warm sauce over pudding.
6 servings.

Eggnog Tarts

CRUSTS
1 (15-ounce) package refrigerated pie crusts
1 teaspoon flour

FILLING
1 (3⅛-ounce) package vanilla pudding and pie filling mix (not instant)
1 cup dairy eggnog (not canned)
1 cup milk

GARNISH
¼ cup whipping cream, whipped
Nutmeg

Allow 1 crust pouch to stand at room temperature for 15 to 20 minutes. (Refrigerate remaining crust for a later use.) Heat oven to 450°F. Unfold pie crust; peel off top plastic sheet. Press out fold lines; sprinkle flour over crust. Cut five 4-inch circles from crust. Fit circles, flour side down, over backs of ungreased muffin cups. Pinch 5 equally spaced pleats around sides of each cup. Prick each crust generously with fork. Bake at 450°F. for 9 to 13 minutes or until light golden brown. Cool completely; remove from muffin cups.

In small saucepan, combine pudding mix, eggnog and milk. Cook over medium heat until mixture comes to a boil, stirring constantly. Cover with plastic wrap; cool completely. Spoon generous ⅓ cup mixture into each cooled crust. Refrigerate until thoroughly chilled. Just before serving, garnish each tart with dollop of whipped cream and dash of nutmeg.
5 tarts.

Cranberry Pudding with Butter Sauce

Bread crumbs are the secret ingredient for the rich, dense texture of this delicious pudding. The other exciting feature is that this is microwaved in less than 15 minutes versus hours of stovetop steaming. With the Butter Sauce, our tasters couldn't stop eating this wonderful creation.

COOK'S NOTE

Whipping Cream
Real whipped cream is a special addition for many desserts. To whip cream, chill the bowl and beaters. Whip cream as close to the serving time as convenient. Whip only until soft peaks form, using care not to whip beyond this point. To sweeten whipped cream, add 1 to 2 tablespoons powdered sugar just before whipping is completed. The cornstarch in the powdered sugar helps to stabilize the whipped cream.

Warm Cranberry Alexander

1½ cups cranberry juice cocktail
¾ cup white crème de cacao
6 tablespoons whipped cream

Heat cranberry juice in small saucepan until very hot. Remove from heat; stir in crème de cacao. Pour into 6 heat-proof glasses. Gently place 1 tablespoon whipped cream on surface of each warm drink. Serve immediately. **6 servings.**

MICROWAVE DIRECTIONS: In 2-cup microwave-safe measuring cup, microwave cranberry juice on HIGH for 3 to 4 minutes or until very hot. Continue as directed above.

NUTRITION INFORMATION PER SERVING

Serving Size: ⅙ of recipe		Percent U.S. RDA	
		Protein	*
Calories	160	Vitamin A	2%
Protein	0g	Vitamin C	25%
Carbohydrate	20g	Thiamine	*
Fat	3g	Riboflavin	*
Cholesterol	10mg	Niacin	*
Sodium	0mg	Calcium	*
Potassium	15mg	Iron	*
		*Contains less than 2%	

Warm Blueberry Sipper

3 cups water
2 cups fresh or frozen blueberries
½ cup sugar
2 lemon slices, ¼ inch thick
1 cinnamon stick
1 tablespoon cornstarch
¼ cup cold water
Whipped cream, if desired

In medium saucepan, combine 3 cups water, blueberries, sugar, lemon slices and cinnamon stick; bring to a boil. Reduce heat; simmer 10 minutes or until blueberries are soft. Remove lemon slices and cinnamon stick. Pour blueberry mixture into blender container or food processor bowl with metal blade; blend until smooth.* Return to saucepan. In small bowl, combine cornstarch and ¼ cup water; stir into blueberry mixture. Cook over medium heat until mixture boils and slightly thickens, stirring constantly. Boil 1 minute, stirring constantly. Pour into 8 heatproof glasses. Gently place dollop of whipped cream on surface of each warm drink. Serve immediately. **8 servings.**

MICROWAVE DIRECTIONS: In 8-cup microwave-safe measuring cup, combine 3 cups water, blueberries, sugar, lemon slices and cinnamon stick. Microwave on HIGH for 12 to 13 minutes or until mixture boils. Microwave on HIGH for an additional 3 to 4 minutes or until blueberries are soft. Remove lemon slices and cinnamon stick. Pour blueberry mixture into blender container or food processor bowl with metal blade; blend until smooth.* Return to measuring cup. In small bowl, combine cornstarch and ¼ cup water; stir into blueberry mixture. Microwave on HIGH for 3 to 4 minutes or until mixture boils and slightly thickens, stirring once during cooking.

TIP: *If using blender with small container, blend ½ mixture at a time.

NUTRITION INFORMATION PER SERVING

Serving Size: ⅛ of recipe		Percent U.S. RDA	
		Protein	*
Calories	100	Vitamin A	2%
Protein	0g	Vitamin C	6%
Carbohydrate	19g	Thiamine	*
Fat	3g	Riboflavin	*
Cholesterol	10mg	Niacin	*
Sodium	5mg	Calcium	*
Potassium	40mg	Iron	*
		*Contains less than 2%	

Warm Blueberry Sipper

This warm fruit drink is a Scandinavian favorite. Enjoy it outdoors on a ski outing or at home after returning.

COOK'S NOTE

Hot Beverage Garnishes

Add a special touch to your beverages with a festive garnish. For hot beverages choose any of these:
• Chocolate curls
• Chocolate shavings
• Cinnamon sticks
• Lemon, lime or orange slices studded with cloves
• Citrus wedges, twists or knots

Pictured left to right: Warm Blueberry Sipper; Warm Cranberry Alexander

# A Children's Christmas

Recipes for Young Ones to Make, Give & Enjoy

When the snow piles deep or rain washes the windows, there's nothing like an afternoon or evening in the kitchen to vanquish kids' "When's Christmas coming?" anticipation. So this Christmas season, instead of shooing your children out of the kitchen, entice them into it. Surrounded by spices and sprinkles, flour and sugars, raisins and nuts, chocolate and chips, they'll revel in the delightful aromas and love helping create Christmas foods.

In these selected-for-kids recipes, you'll find some, such as Honey-Glazed Munch Mix, that children can make easily on their own, using simple utensils, a minimum of ingredients and either the microwave or no oven at all. Others, including Crescent Christmas Tree, will require your supervision and assistance. And still others, like Jolly Santa Lollipops, are just plain fun for kids to eat. Great gifts for them to make and give include Fido's Favorite Treats and Rudolph Cookie Pops.

When choosing recipes for kids, remember to select ones that are appropriate for their age. Teens can tackle Honey Bear Breads, and grade-schoolers can stir up Pat-in-Pan Peanut Butter Fudge. But even the tiniest tots can lend a hand decorating Frosty the Popcorn Man and Jolly Old St. Nick Cake. And the whole family can help assemble Santa's Gingerbread Bake Shoppe or the Sugar Cube Castle.

During Christmas vacation, the kitchen's a great place to sneak in a little education. Use measurements as a refresher course in fractions and reading the recipe as an exercise in following directions. These recipes are also good as a holiday-season activity for a play group or Scout troop.

Before you turn kids loose in the kitchen, consider the following tips to make the experience both safe and enjoyable. Encourage them to:
• Wash their hands.
• Get out all equipment before beginning to cook.
• Use pot holders when handling hot cookie sheets.
• Use knives with a cutting board; cut away from themselves.
• Turn handles of saucepans toward the center of the range.
• Clean up dishes and ingredients after baking.

Pictured on preceding pages: Orange Cinnamon Sugar Cookies with Potato Printing on Cookies and Cookie Paints.

Orange Cinnamon Sugar Cookies

1¼ cups powdered sugar
 1 cup margarine or butter, softened
1½ teaspoons grated orange peel
 1 egg
2½ cups all purpose or unbleached flour
 1 teaspoon baking soda
 1 teaspoon cream of tartar
 ½ teaspoon cinnamon

In large bowl, beat sugar and margarine until light and fluffy. Add orange peel and egg; blend well. Lightly spoon flour into measuring cup; level off. Stir in flour, baking soda, cream of tartar and cinnamon; mix well. Cover with plastic wrap; refrigerate 1 hour for easier handling.

Heat oven to 375°F. On lightly floured surface, roll out ⅓ of dough at a time to ⅛-inch thickness. (Refrigerate remaining dough.) Cut with floured 2-inch round or desired shaped cookie cutter. Place 1 inch apart on ungreased cookie sheets.* Bake at 375°F. for 6 to 9 minutes or until edges are light golden brown. Immediately remove from cookie sheets; cool completely.
5 dozen cookies.

TIPS: *If decorating with Cookie Paints or Potato Printing on Cookies, apply before baking.

To make Christmas Card Cookies, see directions on page 10.

HIGH ALTITUDE — Above 3500 Feet: Decrease powdered sugar to 1 cup. Bake as directed above.

VARIATION:
VANILLA SUGAR COOKIES: Omit orange peel and cinnamon; add 1 teaspoon vanilla.

NUTRITION INFORMATION PER SERVING

Serving Size: 1 Orange, Cinnamon Sugar Cookie		Percent U.S. RDA	
Calories	60	Protein	*
Protein	1g	Vitamin A	2%
Carbohydrate	6g	Vitamin C	*
Fat	3g	Thiamine	2%
Cholesterol	4mg	Riboflavin	*
Sodium	55mg	Niacin	*
Potassium	10mg	Calcium	*
		Iron	*
		*Contains less than 2%	

Potato Printing on Cookies

Prepare dough for Orange Cinnamon Sugar Cookies. Roll and cut out as directed; place on ungreased cookie sheets. Cut medium-sized raw potato in half crosswise. Using small cookie or canapé cutter, push cutter into cut side of potato ¼ to ½ inch deep. Using knife, trim potato away from outside of cutter; remove cutter. Repeat to make another design on remaining potato half. Place 1 tablespoon evaporated milk on small plate. Add several drops desired food color; mix well. Place potato, design side down, in evaporated milk mixture. Print design on unbaked cookie. If necessary, evenly distribute evaporated milk mixture over design. Repeat process to imprint remaining cookies. Occasionally blot potato on paper towel. Bake cookies as directed in recipe.

Cookie Paints

Prepare dough for Orange Cinnamon Sugar Cookies. Roll and cut out as directed; place on ungreased cookie sheets. Place 2 tablespoons evaporated milk in each of 4 custard cups. Add 3 to 5 drops desired food color to each cup; mix well. Paint mixture on unbaked cut-out cookies. Bake cookies as directed in recipe.

Frosty the Popcorn Man

Frosty the Popcorn Man

12 cups popped popcorn
⅓ cup margarine or butter
3 cups miniature marshmallows
   Assorted candies or icing
   Ribbon

Place popcorn in large bowl or container. In large saucepan over medium heat, melt margarine and marshmallows, stirring frequently. Cook 2 minutes. Remove from heat. Pour evenly over popcorn; stir quickly to coat. With buttered or wet hands, quickly shape popcorn into one 4-inch and one 6-inch ball.* Flatten 1 side of 6-inch ball and place on waxed paper. Top with 4-inch ball to form head. Decorate as desired.
1 popcorn man.

TIP: *Popcorn mixture can be divided in half and shaped into 2 smaller popcorn men. Shape 4-inch ball for base and 3-inch ball for head. Decorate as desired.
2 popcorn men.

NUTRITION INFORMATION: Variables in this recipe make it impossible to calculate nutrition information.

Frosty the Popcorn Man

This snowman won't melt away, but we guarantee he'll disappear.

Jolly Old St. Nick Cake

Jolly Old St. Nick Cake

CAKE
1 package pudding-included cake mix (any flavor)

FROSTING AND DECORATIONS
1 can ready-to-spread vanilla frosting
1 drop red food color
  Miniature marshmallows
¼ teaspoon red food color
  Gumdrops
  String licorice

Heat oven to 350°F. Grease and flour 13 × 9-inch pan. Prepare and bake cake mix according to package directions. Cool completely.

Stir 1 drop food color into frosting. Reserve ¼ cup of the frosting. Frost top of cake with remaining frosting.

To make Santa's face and hat, arrange 7 marshmallows in upper left corner of cake to form tassel of hat. Using toothpick, outline hat shape on frosted cake. Stir ¼ teaspoon food color into reserved frosting; frost hat. Arrange marshmallows to form brim of hat, beard around face and mustache. (Marshmallow beard will extend to bottom of cake.) Decorate face as desired with gumdrops and string licorice. **12 servings.**

HIGH ALTITUDE — Above 3500 Feet: See cake mix package for directions.

NUTRITION INFORMATION PER SERVING

Serving Size: ¹⁄₁₂ of recipe using devil's food cake mix		Percent U.S. RDA	
Calories	480	Protein	6%
		Vitamin A	*
		Vitamin C	*
Protein	4g	Thiamine	6%
Carbohydrate	72g	Riboflavin	6%
Fat	20g	Niacin	4%
Cholesterol	53mg	Calcium	10%
Sodium	420mg	Iron	6%
Potassium	190mg	*Contains less than 2%	

Cream Cheese Cookie Puzzles

½ cup sugar
½ cup margarine or butter, softened
1 (3-ounce) package cream cheese, softened
1 teaspoon vanilla
½ teaspoon almond, lemon or rum extract
1 egg, separated
2 cups all purpose or unbleached flour
½ teaspoon salt
½ teaspoon water
  Assorted food color

Heat oven to 350°F. In large bowl, combine sugar, margarine and cream cheese; beat well. Add vanilla, almond extract and 1 egg white; blend well. Lightly spoon flour into measuring cup; level off. Stir in flour and salt; mix well. Divide dough in half. On ungreased cookie sheet, press half of dough into a 10 × 8-inch rectangle.

In small bowl, combine reserved egg yolk and water. Divide into several small custard cups or bowls. Add food color to each to make several assorted colors. Using paintbrushes, paint design on dough rectangle with egg yolk paints. Bake at 350°F. for 9 to 15 minutes or until edges are set but not browned. Immediately cut rectangle with sharp knife into several pieces of varying shapes and sizes. Cool 5 minutes; remove from cookie sheet. Repeat with remaining half of dough.
2 cookie puzzles.

HIGH ALTITUDE — Above 3500 Feet: No change.

NUTRITION INFORMATION: Variables in this recipe make it impossible to calculate nutrition information.

Jolly Old St. Nick Cake

What a great idea for a children's Christmas party! Or serve it as dessert for a family meal.

COOK'S NOTE

Cream Cheese

Cream cheese can easily be softened in the microwave oven for ease in spreading or blending with other ingredients. Remove cream cheese from foil package and place on microwave-safe plate. Microwave 8 ounces of cream cheese on MEDIUM for 1 to 1½ minutes or until softened. If cream cheese starts to melt, remove from microwave and let stand until soft.

Santa's Gingerbread Bake Shoppe

Santa's Gingerbread Bake Shoppe

Santa's Gingerbread Bake Shoppe

If you've never made a gingerbread house, this recipe is designed for you. You'll find the pattern on page 140. We've kept it simple but charming and added a few new touches. You may want to prepare the dough early in the day, then bake and assemble it later.

1¼ cups firmly packed brown sugar
¾ cup margarine or butter, softened
½ cup molasses
1 egg
3½ cups all purpose or unbleached flour
2 teaspoons baking soda
1 teaspoon salt
1 teaspoon cinnamon
1 teaspoon ginger
Yellow and pink clear hard candies, crushed (approximately 2 tablespoons yellow and 1 tablespoon pink)
1 (15 × 15-inch) heavy cardboard covered with foil
Decorator Frosting
Milk
Powdered sugar
Assorted candies
Votive candle

In large bowl, beat brown sugar and margarine until light and fluffy. Add molasses and egg; blend well. Lightly spoon flour into measuring cup; level off. Stir in 1 cup flour, baking soda, salt, cinnamon and ginger. Add remaining flour; mix well. Cover with plastic wrap; refrigerate 4 to 6 hours.

Trace pattern pieces on page 140 and cut from heavy paper or light cardboard. Lightly grease 3 cookie sheets. Line 1 greased cookie sheet with foil, keeping foil very smooth. Heat oven to 350°F. Using stockinette-covered or lightly floured rolling pin, roll ⅓ of dough to 15 × 8-inch rectangle, ⅛ inch thick, on foil-lined cookie sheet. Lightly flour dough to prevent pattern pieces from sticking. Refrigerate remaining dough. Place both END pattern pieces on dough 1 inch apart. Cut around pattern pieces with sharp knife or pizza cutter. Cut out windows and heart shape in front END piece; fill each opening with crushed candy (yellow for windows and pink for heart). Cut out light access in back END piece; *Do not fill with candy.* Remove pattern pieces.

Bake at 350°F. for 8 to 12 minutes or until firm to touch. Remove from oven. Immediately reposition END pattern pieces on baked dough and trim to straighten edges. Let candy windows and heart cool and harden, about 1 to 2 minutes. Carefully remove END pieces from cookie sheet; peel off foil. Cool completely.

Roll half of remaining dough on greased cookie sheet as directed above; cut out 1 ROOF and 1 SIDE piece. Using tip of spoon, press indentations into ROOF piece to resemble curved shingles. Bake as directed above, trimming SIDE piece but not ROOF piece. Repeat with remaining dough to make second ROOF and SIDE pieces. Form dough trimmings into ball; roll out. Cut out trees and reindeer using cookie cutters; cut out sign using SIGN pattern. Bake as directed above. Cool completely.

To assemble house: Place Decorator Frosting in decorating bag with desired tip. (A number 7 writing tip works well.) Pipe door and shutter decorations onto front of house. Let dry completely.

Generously pipe frosting along back edge of SIDE wall. Press to adjacent END piece, with SIDE wall just inside END wall. Make sure corners are square. Hold gently until set. Place on foil-covered cardboard. Repeat with remaining SIDE wall. Pipe frosting along front edge of SIDE walls; attach remaining END piece, pressing lightly. Pipe frosting along inside seams to reinforce. Let dry.

Generously pipe frosting around top edge of house. Place ROOF pieces in place, making sure shingles are going in the right direction. Hold until set. Pipe frosting down center of ROOF to reinforce. Brush ROOF with milk; lightly dust with powdered sugar. Decorate house with assorted candies as desired.

Trees and reindeer: Place baked cutout shapes in small amount of frosting on foil-lined cardboard; hold gently until set. If desired, cut trees in half vertically; trim base of tree to form flat edge. Pipe frosting on cut side of 4 pieces. Position pieces at right angles and hold until set. Decorate as desired.

Sign: Write SANTA'S BAKE SHOPPE on SIGN with frosting. Let dry. Prop SIGN against tree or house.

Place votive candle inside house through back opening. *Do not leave gingerbread house unattended while lit.*

Decorator Frosting

2 egg whites
½ teaspoon cream of tartar
2 cups powdered sugar
¼ to ½ teaspoon vanilla,
   peppermint or mint extract
2 to 3 drops food color, if desired

In small bowl, beat egg whites with cream of tartar until soft peaks form. Gradually beat in powdered sugar and vanilla until frosting is smooth and stiff enough to hold firm peaks. Add food color; mix well. Keep frosting covered with damp paper towels while assembling Santa's Gingerbread Bake Shoppe.

1¾ cups.

TIP: We are using this recipe for frosting even though it contains raw egg whites. It sets up quickly, dries very hard and keeps well. There is a possibility of raw eggs being contaminated with salmonella. Therefore, we do not recommend that this be eaten.

Pat-in-Pan Peanut Butter Fudge

Pat-in-Pan Peanut Butter Fudge

Make plenty of no-cook candy for holiday entertaining. Decorate these creamy candies and give them to special friends.

Confetti Popcorn Bars

The ever-popular marshmallow and cereal bars have been updated, using microwave popcorn, candy and peanuts.

½ cup creamy peanut butter
1 (8-ounce) package cream cheese
1 (6-ounce) package (1 cup) peanut butter chips
4 cups powdered sugar

Line 13 × 9-inch pan with foil so that foil extends over sides of pan. In large saucepan, combine peanut butter, cream cheese and peanut butter chips. Heat just until melted and mixture is smooth, stirring constantly. Remove from heat. Add powdered sugar 1 cup at a time, mixing well after each addition; knead if necessary. Press mixture evenly in foil-lined pan. Let stand at room temperature until set, about 2 hours. Remove fudge from pan by lifting foil; remove foil from sides of fudge. Cut into squares or desired shapes. Decorate as desired. Store in refrigerator.

About 2 pounds.

MICROWAVE DIRECTIONS: In 1½-quart microwave-safe bowl, combine peanut butter, cream cheese and peanut butter chips. Microwave on HIGH for 1½ to 3 minutes or until mixture is melted; blend well. (Mixture will be very thick and quite dry-looking.) Continue as directed above.

VARIATION:
PAT-IN-PAN CHOCOLATE FUDGE: Substitute ½ cup margarine or butter for the peanut butter and 3 ounces (3 squares) unsweetened chocolate for the peanut butter chips. Increase powdered sugar to 6 cups. Prepare as directed above except refrigerate to set.
About 2½ pounds.

NUTRITION INFORMATION PER SERVING

Serving Size: 1 ounce Peanut Butter Fudge		Percent U.S. RDA	
Calories	120	Protein	4%
Protein	3g	Vitamin A	2%
Carbohydrate	16g	Vitamin C	*
Fat	6g	Thiamine	*
Cholesterol	8mg	Riboflavin	*
Sodium	55mg	Niacin	4%
Potassium	65mg	Calcium	*
		Iron	*
*Contains less than 2%			

Confetti Popcorn Bars

10 cups popped corn
½ cup candy-coated chocolate pieces or small gumdrops
⅓ cup unsalted peanuts
3 tablespoons margarine or butter
2 cups miniature marshmallows

MICROWAVE DIRECTIONS: Grease 8- or 9-inch square pan and large bowl. In large greased bowl, combine popcorn, candy and peanuts. Place margarine and marshmallows in 4-cup microwave-safe measuring cup. Microwave on HIGH for 1½ to 2 minutes or until melted and smooth, stirring once halfway through cooking. Pour over popcorn mixture; stir quickly to coat. With buttered or wet hands, press mixture into greased pan. Refrigerate until firm. Cut into bars.

16 bars.

VARIATION:
CONFETTI POPCORN BALLS: Prepare mixture as directed above. With buttered or wet hands, quickly shape mixture into 2½- to 3-inch balls. Place on waxed paper. Let stand at room temperature 1 hour. Wrap each ball in plastic wrap.

NUTRITION INFORMATION PER SERVING

Serving Size: 1 bar		Percent U.S. RDA	
Calories	120	Protein	2%
Protein	2g	Vitamin A	*
Carbohydrate	13g	Vitamin C	*
Fat	7g	Thiamine	*
Cholesterol	0mg	Riboflavin	*
Sodium	100mg	Niacin	2%
Potassium	40mg	Calcium	*
		Iron	2%
*Contains less than 2%			

Pictured top to bottom: Honey-Glazed Munch Mix; Confetti Popcorn Bars

Honey-Glazed Munch Mix

5 cups popped popcorn
2 cups crisp corn-rice hexagon-
   shaped cereal
½ cup peanuts
¼ cup raisins
¼ cup honey
¼ cup margarine or butter
¼ teaspoon vanilla

MICROWAVE DIRECTIONS: In large microwave-safe bowl, combine popcorn, cereal, peanuts and raisins; set aside. In 2-cup microwave-safe measuring cup, combine honey, margarine and vanilla. Microwave on HIGH for 45 to 60 seconds; stir until margarine is melted. Drizzle over popcorn mixture; stir quickly to coat. Microwave on MEDIUM for 6 to 7 minutes or until popcorn is crisp, stirring every 2 minutes. Spread on foil; cool completely. Store in loosely covered container. **7 cups.**

NUTRITION INFORMATION PER SERVING

Serving Size: 1 cup		Percent U.S. RDA	
Calories	260	Protein	6%
Protein	5g	Vitamin A	6%
Carbohydrate	34g	Vitamin C	10%
Fat	12g	Thiamine	15%
Cholesterol	0mg	Riboflavin	2%
Sodium	260mg	Niacin	20%
Potassium	150mg	Calcium	*
		Iron	8%
		*Contains less than 2%	

Honey-Glazed Munch Mix

Holiday tree-trimming wouldn't be complete without a snack and warm beverage. Serve this honey-glazed treat with a mug of hot cider or cocoa.

Honey Bear Breads

Honey Bear Breads

BREAD

6 to 6½ cups all purpose or
   unbleached flour
½ cup sugar
¼ cup unsweetened cocoa
1 teaspoon salt
½ teaspoon cinnamon
2 packages active dry yeast
1 cup milk
½ cup warm water
½ cup margarine or butter
1 teaspoon vanilla
3 eggs

GLAZE

¼ cup margarine or butter
2 tablespoons honey

DECORATION

Assorted candies, chocolate
   chips, raisins or icing
Ribbon

Grease 2 large cookie sheets. Lightly spoon flour into measuring cup; level off. In large bowl, combine 2 cups flour, sugar, cocoa, salt, cinnamon and yeast; blend well. In small saucepan, heat milk, water and ½ cup margarine until very warm (120 to 130°F.). Add warm liquid, vanilla and eggs to flour mixture. Blend at low speed until moistened; beat 2 minutes at medium speed. By hand, stir in an additional 3 cups flour to form a stiff dough. On floured surface, knead in remaining 1 to 1½ cups flour until dough is smooth and elastic, about 5 minutes. Place dough in greased bowl; cover loosely with plastic wrap and cloth towel. Let rise in warm place (80 to 85°F.) until light and doubled in size, about 1 hour.

Punch down dough several times to remove all air bubbles. To form 4 bears, divide dough into 4 equal parts. To shape each bear, divide 1 part in half. Shape 1 half into smooth oval ball for bear's body; place on greased cookie sheet. Cut remaining half of dough into 2 equal parts. Pinch two 1-inch balls from 1 part for bear's ears; shape remaining dough into smooth round ball for bear's head and attach to body. Flatten 1-inch balls for ears and position on head. Cut remaining part of dough into 4 equal pieces; shape into arms and legs and attach to bear's body. Cover; let rise in warm place until light and doubled in size, about 30 to 45 minutes.

Heat oven to 350°F. Uncover dough. Bake at 350°F. for 15 to 20 minutes. Meanwhile, in small bowl combine margarine and honey. Remove breads from oven; brush generously with glaze. Return to oven and bake an additional 5 to 7 minutes or until glaze is set and loaves sound hollow when lightly tapped. Cool 5 minutes. Remove from cookie sheets; cool on wire racks. Decorate as desired with assorted candies; tie ribbon bow around neck.
4 breads; 4 servings each.

HIGH ALTITUDE — Above 3500 Feet: No change.

NUTRITION INFORMATION PER SERVING

Serving Size: 1/16 of recipe		Percent U.S. RDA	
		Protein	10%
Calories	330	Vitamin A	8%
Protein	7g	Vitamin C	*
Carbohydrate	51g	Thiamine	30%
Fat	11g	Riboflavin	20%
Cholesterol	41mg	Niacin	15%
Sodium	270mg	Calcium	4%
Potassium	120mg	Iron	15%
		*Contains less than 2%	

Honey Bear Breads

Children will love to receive one of these precious breads!

Rudolph Cookie Pops

Refrigerated cookie dough is cut into geometric shapes that are arranged to create Rudolph. Lightly dust fingers with flour if dough becomes sticky.

Lollipop Place Cards

Jolly Santa Lollipops can be used as perky place cards. To make them, you will need triangular strips of paper or ribbon, glue and paper or Styrofoam cups. For each place card, glue or tie a strip of paper with a name on it to each lollipop stick. Or tie a ribbon around each stick just below the lollipop and glue paper with the name on it to the end of the ribbon. Insert each lollipop stick into an inverted cup. Stand a Jolly Santa Lollipop place card by each place setting.

Cookie Place Card Stand-Ups

For place card stand-ups, prepare dough for one of the cutout cookie recipes. Cut rolled dough with cookie cutters of desired shapes, making sure shape has a straight lower edge. (You will need 2 cookies of the same shape for each place card.) With drinking straw, punch hole in top of each cookie. Bake as directed in recipe. Using tinted frosting, pipe name and decorate half of cooled cookies. With ⅛-inch-wide ribbon, loosely tie decorated cookie to plain cookie of same shape, decorated side out. Repeat with remaining cookies. Stand decorated cookie place card by each place setting.

Apple Santas

To make these delightful party favors or place card holders, you will need medium shiny red apples, large marshmallows, raisins, red chewy fruit rolls, corn syrup, toothpicks and a small amount of cotton. For each Santa, attach marshmallow arms, legs and head to an apple with toothpicks. Add raisin eyes and nose and a peaked cap made from the fruit roll. Using corn syrup, attach a cotton beard and trim. If necessary, prop the apple in back with a toothpick.

Rudolph Cookie Pops

1 (20-ounce) package refrigerated
   sliceable sugar cookies
32 to 36 wooden sticks
   Frosting tinted as desired
   Round red candy

Freeze cookie dough at least 1 hour. Heat oven to 350°F. Cut frozen dough into ¼-inch slices. (Return rest of dough to freezer while shaping cookies on sheet.) Use 1 slice to shape each reindeer. Cut 2 strips off sides of each slice of dough, forming a triangle. Place triangles on ungreased cookie sheet 3 inches apart and 2 inches from edges of sheet. Cut 1 strip into 2 small pieces for ears. Attach pieces to head and shape to form ears. Cut second strip into 2 pieces and roll into two 1-inch long ropes. Attach between ears to form antlers. (See diagram.) Securely insert a wooden stick into nose end of each cookie, with free end of stick pointing toward center of cookie sheet. Bake at 350°F. for 8 to 12 minutes or until golden brown. Cool 2 minutes; remove from cookie sheet with wide spatula. Cool completely. Frost or decorate as desired, using red candy for nose. Let stand until frosting is set. Store in loosely covered container. **About 3 dozen cookies.**

NUTRITION INFORMATION PER SERVING

Serving Size: 1 cookie		Percent U.S. RDA	
Calories	70	Protein	*
Protein	1g	Vitamin A	*
Carbohydrate	11g	Vitamin C	*
Fat	3g	Thiamine	*
Cholesterol	2mg	Riboflavin	*
Sodium	65mg	Niacin	2%
Potassium	10mg	Calcium	*
		Iron	*
*Contains less than 2%			

Diagrams for Rudolph Cookie Pops

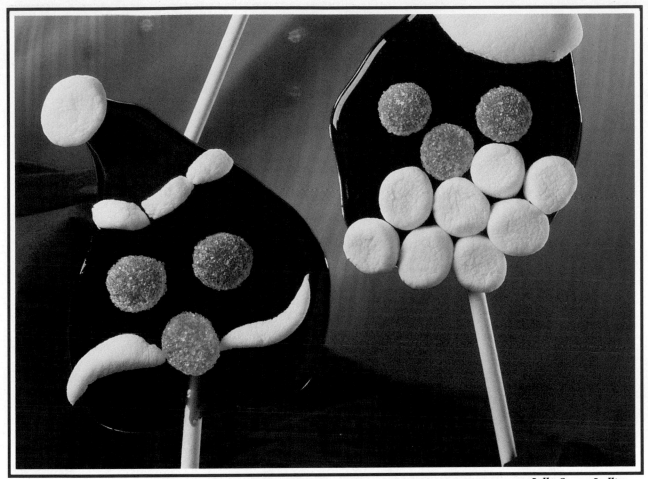
Jolly Santa Lollipops

Jolly Santa Lollipops

12 lollipop sticks
1 cup sugar
½ cup light corn syrup
¼ cup water
1 to 2 teaspoons cherry extract*
⅛ to ¼ teaspoon red food color
2 large marshmallows
4 gumdrops

Line 2 cookie sheets with foil, keeping foil very smooth. Place lollipop sticks 4 inches apart on cookie sheets. In medium saucepan, combine sugar, corn syrup and water. Cook, stirring constantly until sugar dissolves. Cook without stirring until candy thermometer reaches 290°F. (soft-crack stage). Remove from heat. Immediately stir in cherry extract and red food color. Using about 1 tablespoon of syrup for each lollipop, quickly spoon syrup over sticks, shaping into round head with peaked cap.** Let cool and harden.

Remove from foil. With scissors, cut marshmallows into strips and gumdrops into pieces or slices. Place cut sides down on lollipops to create Santa faces.

12 lollipops.

TIPS: *One teaspoon peppermint extract or 4 to 5 teaspoons raspberry extract can be substituted for cherry extract.

**If syrup becomes too stiff, return to low heat until thin enough to spoon.

NUTRITION INFORMATION PER SERVING

Serving Size: 1 lollipop		Percent U.S. RDA	
Calories	110	Protein	*
Protein	0g	Vitamin A	*
Carbohydrate	28g	Vitamin C	*
Fat	0g	Thiamine	*
Cholesterol	0mg	Riboflavin	*
Sodium	10mg	Niacin	*
Potassium	0mg	Calcium	*
		Iron	2%
		*Contains less than 2%	

Jolly Santa Lollipops

Wrap these charming pops in plastic wrap, tie with a bow and have ready to give to visiting youngsters.

Crescent Christmas Tree

Crescent Christmas Tree

Here's a festive holiday bread you can make without spending hours in the kitchen, thanks to refrigerated crescent roll dough.

Fido's Favorite Treats

Give a package of these canine treats to your favorite dog. Include a bone-shaped cutter and a copy of the recipe for the dog's owner.

BREAD
  2 (8-ounce) cans refrigerated
    crescent dinner rolls
  2 tablespoons margarine or butter,
    softened
  2 tablespoons sugar
  1 teaspoon cinnamon

GLAZE
  ½ cup powdered sugar
  1 tablespoon milk
  ¼ teaspoon vanilla

GARNISH
  Red and green candied cherries,
    halved

Heat oven to 375°F. Lightly grease cookie sheet. Separate dough into 4 rectangles. Firmly press perforations to seal. Spread each rectangle with margarine. In small bowl, combine sugar and cinnamon; sprinkle evenly over rectangles. Starting at shorter side, roll up each rectangle; seal edge. Cut each roll crosswise into 3 equal slices. Place slices cut side down on greased cookie sheet to form tree. Begin with 1 slice for top; arrange 2 slices just below, with sides closely touching. Continue arranging a row of 3 slices, then a row of 4 slices. Use the remaining 2 slices for the trunk. Bake at 375°F. for 15 to 20 minutes or until deep golden brown. Cool 3 minutes; carefully remove from cookie sheet. Cool slightly on wire rack.

In small bowl, combine glaze ingredients until smooth; drizzle over tree. Garnish with candied cherry halves.
12 rolls.

NUTRITION INFORMATION PER SERVING

Serving Size: 1 roll		Percent U.S. RDA	
Calories	180	Protein	4%
Protein	2g	Vitamin A	*
Carbohydrate	22g	Vitamin C	*
Fat	9g	Thiamine	6%
Cholesterol	4mg	Riboflavin	4%
Sodium	330mg	Niacin	4%
Potassium	90mg	Calcium	*
		Iron	4%
*Contains less than 2%			

Fido's Favorite Treats

  1 cup rolled oats
  ⅓ cup margarine
  1 cup boiling water
  ¾ cup cornmeal
  1 tablespoon sugar
  1 to 2 teaspoons chicken- or beef-
    flavored instant bouillon
  ½ cup milk
  4 ounces (1 cup) shredded
    Cheddar cheese
  1 egg, beaten
  2 to 3 cups all purpose or whole
    wheat flour

Heat oven to 325°F. Grease cookie sheets. In large bowl, combine rolled oats, margarine and boiling water; let stand 10 minutes. Stir in cornmeal, sugar, bouillon, milk, cheese and egg; mix well. Lightly spoon flour into measuring cup; level off. Add flour 1 cup at a time, mixing well after each addition to form a stiff dough. On floured surface, knead in remaining flour until dough is smooth and no longer sticky, 3 to 4 minutes. Roll or pat out dough to ½-inch thickness; cut with bone-shaped cookie cutter. Place 1 inch apart on greased cookie sheets. Bake at 325°F. for 35 to 45 minutes or until golden brown. Cool completely. Store loosely covered.
3½ dozen large dog biscuits or 8 dozen small dog biscuits.

HIGH ALTITUDE—Above 3500 Feet: No change.

NUTRITION INFORMATION: Not applicable.

Sugar Cube Castle

Sugar Cube Castle

1 (15 × 15-inch) heavy cardboard
  covered with foil
4 (1-pound) boxes sugar cocktail
  cubes
1 can ready-to-spread vanilla
  frosting
  Assorted candies
  Votive candle

Centered on cardboard, arrange single
layer of sugar cubes (about 15 per side)
to make 8 × 8-inch square; leave 7-
cube space for door. Continue to build,
layer by layer, spreading or piping frosting to hold cubes and layers together.
As walls are built up, leave spaces for
windows. Support tops of windows and
doors with strips of heavy paper cut
slightly longer than opening. Build tow-
ers in corners. Use additional cubes to
make door and various other decorations on and around castle. Decorate
with candies as desired. Place votive
candle in center. *Do not leave castle unattended while lit.*

Home for the Holidays

Festive Feasts Great & Small

With the coming of Christmas, our hearts and our homes are opened to loved ones, both family and friends. Maybe it's the special dishes that adorn the table, the same group of smiling faces brought together year after year, the don't-ever-change-it menu, or the only-at-Christmas activities that forge indelible memories to last a lifetime.

The holidays wouldn't be the holidays without entertaining. Yet there is no need to be rushed or frantic. For your feasts great and small, try these simple yet enticing menus. The Company's Coming Open House menu makes serving a crowd a cinch. All the recipes can be doubled or halved depending on the number of guests.

After a Christmas-tree-cutting expedition, invite your friends over for the Fireside Dinner, a warming and hearty soup-and-bread supper that serves 8. Christmas Day is special in so many ways. After the excitement of Santa's arrival, extend the holiday spirit with one of our festive dinners featuring elegant but easy entrees of capon, roast beef or crown roast of pork, each one sure to provide pleasant memories of a special holiday.

So that even Santa's elves can sleep in, serve the make-ahead Christmas Morning Brunch. All the dishes can be made in advance to eliminate that last-minute fuss.

All these menus are flexible. They suggest recipe combinations that work well together, but you may choose to substitute others, mixing and matching them to suit your taste. In some instances you'll need to select companion foods from the breads, desserts, cookies or candies chapters. Just remember when making your choices to keep in mind the number of people each recipe serves.

Holiday decorations that cheerfully light up our homes add greatly to the pleasure of Christmas. Dip into Holiday Trimmings, a section brimming with creative ideas to brighten your home, from candles and Ice Ball Lanterns to special table decorations and Scents of the Holidays.

So whether you're planning to serve 4 or 24, relax, enjoy and celebrate this season of togetherness.

Holiday Trimmings to Brighten Your Home

Holiday Tables

Solid-colored napkins, tablecloths and place mats in any of the holiday colors and/or white can be combined in many ways to make bright, festive table settings without requiring special linens that are stored for the rest of the year. For a large table, try a white or colored sheet with colored napkins (all of one color or a combination). Use ribbon bows for napkin rings or tie ribbons around the stems of goblets.

Holiday Napkin Tie

For each napkin tie, purchase ¾ yard of satin ribbon in ⅜- or ½-inch width. Stitch a small jingle bell to each end of the ribbon. Tie a ribbon around the napkin for each place setting.

Cinnamon Stick Place Card Holders

For each place card holder, use 7 to 9 short cinnamon sticks; tie them into a bundle with a ribbon. Add a sprig of dried baby's breath. Insert a place card into the bundle and set one bundle at each place setting. These small bundles can be given to guests as gifts when they depart.

TIP: Cinnamon sticks can be purchased economically in bulk form at food co-ops and some supermarkets.

Candle Arrangements

Candle arrangements in unusual containers can be creative yet simple, too. Use unusual containers and other items you have around your home. Try votive candles in fluted molds, muffin pans or on inverted clay flower pots in clay saucers and surround with multi-colored jingle bells, small shiny tree ornaments or pine cones. Florist clay or candle "stickem" can be used to secure the candles.

Pictured on preceding pages clockwise from left: Roast Capon with Tarragon, page 105; Praline Sweet Potatoes, page 102; Cranberry-Orange Salad, page 105

Red apples can be made into candle holders by cutting holes in them with an apple corer or paring knife. Insert candles and tie colorful ribbons around them.

Winter Wonderland "Tablescape"

Candles can be used to create an illusion of moonlight on snow-covered boughs. Place white or ivory candles of various heights in glass holders. Group and surround them with snow-flocked evergreens. Intertwine colored or metallic ribbons and place around the candle holders, and add a touch of fantasy with crystal angels, trees or reindeer. For a doubly beautiful display, arrange the grouping against a mirrored background to catch and reflect the light.

Scents of the Holidays

In small saucepan, combine 2 cinnamon sticks, 3 whole cloves, 3 whole allspice and 3 cups water. Bring to a boil; reduce heat. Simmer over low heat. Check mixture periodically and add more water when necessary. Simmer this mixture before guests arrive to fill your home with the scents of the holidays.

Holiday Gift Baskets

Select a basket large enough to hold gift items. Line the basket with small evergreen branches, a holiday napkin, a square of hemmed or fringed counted cross-stitch or embroidery. Place food items in basket and attach a large bow. Copies of the recipes would be most welcome, too!

Chocolate Gift Basket

Place an assortment of chocolate gift items in a basket, such as Apricot Double Dips, Chocolate Praline Ice Cream Topping and Flavored Mocha Mixes.

Muffin Gift Basket

Prepare Holiday Muffin Mix recipe, page 138. Accompany mix with muffin tins, decorative pot holders or other related kitchen items.

Spaghetti Dinner Basket

For the gadget-lover on your gift list, place a jar of Quick Spaghetti Sauce, page 135, in basket; add related food items or kitchen gadgets to complete the basket.

Large Ice Lanterns

To make these lanterns, which originated in the cold and dark winters of Finland, you will need very cold weather (about 0°F. or colder is best), large plastic buckets (2 gallons or larger) and pillar candles.

Fill the buckets with water; allow to stand outdoors overnight. The water will freeze to a thickness of about 2 inches on the sides and at the top. When frozen, invert the buckets and remove from the ice lanterns. The hollow, which was on the bottom and is now on top, is just right for a pillar candle. (If a thin layer of ice has formed over the bottom, break it to find the hollow; drain out the water.)

Paper Bag Luminarias

To make these luminarias, you will need brown, white or colored lunch-sized paper bags (about $10 \times 5 \times 3$ inches), votive or plumber's candles and sand.

If desired, bags can be decorated before opening them to fill with sand. Children can draw or paint designs on the brown or white bags. A paper punch can be used to create a design of holes, or a scissors can be used to cut small snowflake designs in the bags. Keep decorative openings small so the wind cannot blow out the candles. Fold the top of each bag down about 1 inch for additional strength and add about 2 inches of sand. Place a candle in the center of the sand, making sure it does not touch the edges of the bag; light the candle. Place bags 3 to 6 feet apart along edge of sidewalk or yard, or arrange on steps.

CAUTION: Do not place luminarias near dry leaves or shrubbery.

Ice Ball Lanterns

These wonderful lanterns look like illuminated crystal vases when lighted. They will burn up to 12 hours.

For each lantern you will need a 9-inch round balloon, a 5-quart ice cream bucket or similar container and a votive candle. (It is very helpful to have 1 bucket for each lantern.)

Paper Bag Luminarias, Ice Ball Lantern

Fill the balloon with water by stretching the end over a faucet. For ease in handling, hold the balloon over the ice cream bucket as it is being filled. When the balloon is filled to the top, tie it with a knot. Place the balloon, in bucket, in the freezer; freeze at 0°F. for about 12 hours or until about ½ inch of ice has formed all around inside of balloon. (You will not be able to tell for sure how thick the ice is until you have made one lantern.)

Remove from freezer; peel off and discard the balloon. With a serrated knife or small saw blade, cut off the top of the ice ball about 2 inches down, or even with the top of the bucket. Pour out the water. (If ice has started to form throughout the inside of the ball, remove the ice and reduce the freezing time of additional lanterns.) Replace the ice ball in the bucket and return to the freezer, or store outdoors when the temperature is near or below freezing. Repeat to make additional lanterns (or make at the same time if you have the freezer space).

When ready to place the lanterns in position outdoors, light votive candles and, using tongs, place a candle in each lantern. Carry the lantern to position in the bucket, then remove. If lighting candles outdoors, choose a sheltered place.

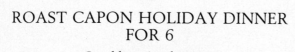

ROAST CAPON HOLIDAY DINNER FOR 6

Sparkling Apple Juice
Cranberry-Orange Salad*
Roast Capon with Tarragon*
Corn Bread Dressing*
Praline Sweet Potatoes*
Buttered Broccoli
Sesame Roll Gifts*
*Recipe Included

Roast Capon with Tarragon

BASTING SAUCE
- ½ cup cream sherry
- ¼ cup margarine or butter
- 2 teaspoons tarragon leaves
- ⅛ teaspoon pepper

CAPON
- 1 (7-pound) capon or large roasting chicken
- Salt
- 1 medium carrot, cut into chunks
- 1 celery stalk, cut into chunks
- 2 shallots, peeled, cut up
- 1 tablespoon tarragon leaves

In small saucepan, boil sherry until reduced to about ¼ cup. Add remaining sauce ingredients.

Heat oven to 325°F. Remove giblets and rinse capon; pat dry. Sprinkle cavity with salt. Fill cavity with carrot, celery, shallots and 1 tablespoon tarragon. Pull skin over neck cavity; fasten with skewer. Tuck legs under or tie together, tucking tail inside. Place capon, breast side up, on rack in roasting pan. Insert meat thermometer into thickest part of thigh next to body cavity, being careful bulb does not rest in fat or on bone. Spoon basting sauce over capon.

Roast at 325°F. for 2½ to 3 hours or until meat thermometer reaches 185°F., basting with sauce every 30 minutes. For ease in carving, let capon stand loosely covered with foil for 15 minutes to set juices. Remove and discard vegetable stuffing.
8 to 10 servings.

TIP: Pan juices can be served with capon. Remove fat and boil vigorously until slightly thickened.

NUTRITION INFORMATION PER SERVING

Serving Size: ⅒ of recipe		Percent U.S. RDA	
Calories	220	Protein	50%
Protein	31g	Vitamin A	2%
Carbohydrate	0g	Vitamin C	*
Fat	9g	Thiamine	4%
Cholesterol	94mg	Riboflavin	10%
Sodium	135mg	Niacin	50%
Potassium	290mg	Calcium	*
		Iron	8%
		*Contains less than 2%	

Sesame Roll Gifts

Sesame Roll Gifts

1 package hot roll mix
1 cup water heated to 120 to
 130°F.
2 tablespoons margarine or butter,
 softened
1 egg

TOPPING
 1 teaspoon water
 1 egg white, slightly beaten
 1 tablespoon sesame seed

 6 yards grosgrain ribbon, ¼ inch
 wide

Grease large cookie sheet. In large bowl, combine flour mixture with yeast from foil packet; blend well. Stir in *hot* water, margarine and 1 egg until dough pulls away from sides of bowl. Turn out onto lightly floured surface. With greased or floured hands, shape dough into a ball. Knead dough for 5 minutes until smooth. Cover with large bowl; let rest 5 minutes.

Divide dough into 32 equal pieces; shape into balls. Place on greased cookie sheet, arranging balls together in groups of 4, sides touching, to form squares. In small bowl, combine 1 teaspoon water and egg white; mix well. Brush over tops of rolls; sprinkle with sesame seed. Cover loosely with plastic wrap and cloth towel. Let rise in warm place (80 to 85°F.) until light and doubled in size, about 30 minutes.

Heat oven to 375°F. Uncover dough. Bake at 375°F. for 18 to 23 minutes or until golden brown. Immediately remove from cookie sheet; cool completely on wire rack. To serve, wrap each roll with ribbon to resemble gift package, ending with a bow on top.
8 rolls.

TIP: To reheat ribbon-tied rolls, wrap loosely in foil; heat at 350°F. about 15 minutes or until warm.

HIGH ALTITUDE – Above 3500 Feet: No change.

NUTRITION INFORMATION PER SERVING

Serving Size: 1 roll		Percent U.S. RDA	
Calories	250	Protein	10%
Protein	8g	Vitamin A	2%
Carbohydrate	42g	Vitamin C	*
Fat	5g	Thiamine	25%
Cholesterol	27mg	Riboflavin	20%
Sodium	440mg	Niacin	15%
Potassium	95mg	Calcium	*
		Iron	10%
		*Contains less than 2%	

Corn Bread

Corn Bread

When baked, about half of this recipe provides the three cups of crumbs needed for Corn Bread Dressing. Serve the remaining bread warm with soup.

Corn Bread Dressing

"Dressing" bakes beside the bird, while "stuffing" bakes inside the bird.

1 cup all purpose or unbleached flour
1 cup cornmeal
2 tablespoons sugar
4 teaspoons baking powder
1 teaspoon salt
1 cup milk
¼ cup oil or melted shortening
1 egg, slightly beaten

Heat oven to 425°F. Grease 8- or 9-inch square pan. Lightly spoon flour into measuring cup; level off. In medium bowl, combine flour, cornmeal, sugar, baking powder and salt. Stir in remaining ingredients, beating by hand *just* until smooth. Pour batter into greased pan. Bake at 425°F. for 18 to 22 minutes or until toothpick inserted in center comes out clean.
9 servings.

HIGH ALTITUDE—Above 3500 Feet: Decrease baking powder to 1½ teaspoons. Bake as directed above.

NUTRITION INFORMATION PER SERVING

Serving Size: ⅑ of recipe		Percent U.S. RDA	
		Protein	6%
Calories	190	Vitamin A	2%
Protein	4g	Vitamin C	*
Carbohydrate	25g	Thiamine	10%
Fat	8g	Riboflavin	10%
Cholesterol	26mg	Niacin	6%
Sodium	400mg	Calcium	10%
Potassium	105mg	Iron	6%
		*Contains less than 2%	

Corn Bread Dressing

¼ cup margarine or butter
½ cup chopped onion
½ cup chopped celery
3 cups Corn Bread crumbs
2 cups dry bread cubes
2 tablespoons chopped fresh parsley
½ to 1 teaspoon sage leaves, crumbled
½ teaspoon salt
1 cup chicken broth
1 egg, beaten

Heat oven to 325°F. Grease 9-inch square pan. Melt margarine in small skillet over medium-high heat. Add onion and celery; cook and stir until tender. In medium bowl, combine cooked onion and celery with remaining ingredients; mix well. Place in greased pan. Bake at 325°F. for 1 hour, occasionally basting with pan juices from Roast Capon with Tarragon.*
8 (½-cup) servings.

TIP: *To bake dressing without capon, bake at 400°F. for 30 minutes.

NUTRITION INFORMATION PER SERVING

Serving Size: ½ cup		Percent U.S. RDA	
Calories	210	Protein	8%
Protein	5g	Vitamin A	8%
Carbohydrate	23g	Vitamin C	2%
Fat	11g	Thiamine	8%
Cholesterol	41mg	Riboflavin	10%
Sodium	610mg	Niacin	8%
Potassium	150mg	Calcium	10%
		Iron	8%

Praline Sweet Potatoes

3 pounds sweet potatoes
⅓ cup sugar
¼ teaspoon nutmeg
¼ cup margarine or butter, melted
⅓ cup milk
1 egg, slightly beaten

PRALINE TOPPING
¼ cup chopped pecans
¼ cup coconut
¼ cup firmly packed brown sugar
2 tablespoons flour
2 tablespoons margarine or butter, melted

Scrub potatoes; cut into quarters. In large saucepan, bring potatoes and enough water to cover to a boil. Reduce heat; cover and simmer 20 to 25 minutes or until tender. Cool slightly; peel potatoes.

Heat oven to 325°F. In medium bowl, mash warm potatoes. Stir in sugar, nutmeg and ¼ cup margarine. In small bowl, combine milk and egg. Add to sweet potato mixture; blend well. Place in ungreased 1½-quart casserole or baking dish. In small bowl, combine all praline topping ingredients; blend well. Sprinkle over sweet potatoes. Bake at 325°F. for 1 hour or until slightly puffed and browned.
8 servings.

MICROWAVE DIRECTIONS: Combine all praline topping ingredients. Set aside. To microwave sweet potatoes, prick potatoes with fork. Place on microwave-safe paper towels. Microwave on HIGH for 15 to 18 minutes or until tender. Let stand 5 to 10 minutes. Peel potatoes. In medium bowl, mash warm potatoes. Stir in sugar, nutmeg and ¼ cup margarine. In small bowl, combine milk and egg. Add to sweet potato mixture; blend well. Place in ungreased 1½-quart microwave-safe casserole or baking dish. Microwave on HIGH for 2 minutes; stir. Sprinkle with topping. Microwave on HIGH for 6 to 8 minutes or until hot.

NUTRITION INFORMATION PER SERVING

Serving Size: ⅛ of recipe		Percent U.S. RDA	
		Protein	6%
Calories	350	Vitamin A	510%
Protein	4g	Vitamin C	30%
Carbohydrate	55g	Thiamine	6%
Fat	13g	Riboflavin	15%
Cholesterol	27mg	Niacin	6%
Sodium	135mg	Calcium	6%
Potassium	350mg	Iron	8%

Cranberry-Orange Salad

1 cup sugar
½ cup chopped walnuts
1 (12-ounce) package fresh or frozen cranberries, finely chopped
1 (11-ounce) can mandarin orange segments, drained
1 (6-ounce) package orange-flavored gelatin
2 cups boiling water
Leaf lettuce

Oil 8 to 10 individual molds or 6-cup mold. In large bowl, combine sugar, walnuts, cranberries and orange segments; set aside. In another large bowl, dissolve gelatin in boiling water. Refrigerate until slightly thickened, about 45 minutes. Stir cranberry-orange mixture into thickened gelatin. Spoon into oiled molds. Refrigerate about 3 hours or until firm. To serve, unmold onto lettuce-lined serving plates. Garnish as desired.
8 to 10 servings.

NUTRITION INFORMATION PER SERVING

Serving Size: ⅒ of recipe		Percent U.S. RDA	
		Protein	4%
Calories	200	Vitamin A	4%
Protein	3g	Vitamin C	15%
Carbohydrate	43g	Thiamine	2%
Fat	4g	Riboflavin	*
Cholesterol	0mg	Niacin	*
Sodium	55mg	Calcium	*
Potassium	125mg	Iron	*
		*Contains less than 2%	

COOK'S NOTE

Choosing Sweet Potatoes

Two types of sweet potatoes are generally available, moist or dry-meated. The moist varieties, sometimes called yams, are sweeter than the dry and are tan to brownish-red in color. The skin of the dry type is usually yellowish tan or fawn-colored.

Regardless of which variety you choose, purchase firm, unbruised smooth-skinned potatoes that taper toward the ends.

BEEF RIB ROAST HOLIDAY DINNER FOR 8

Chilled Eggnog
Jicama Spinach Salad*
Beef Rib Roast*
Horseradish Sauce*
Cheddar Potatoes with Wreath of Vegetables*
Tannenbaum Dinner Rolls
(page 50)
Frozen Cranberry Pie
(page 76)
*Recipe Included

Jicama Spinach Salad

1 medium jicama
10 ounces fresh spinach, torn into bite-sized pieces (8 cups)
1 cup sliced fresh strawberries or seeds of 1 pomegranate

DRESSING
¼ cup lime juice
3 tablespoons honey
2 tablespoons oil

To make jicama cutouts, peel jicama. Cut into ¼-inch slices. Using canapé cutters, cut desired shapes from slices.

In large bowl, gently toss spinach, strawberries and jicama cutouts; refrigerate until serving time. In small bowl, combine all dressing ingredients; blend well. Cover; refrigerate 1 hour to blend flavors. Just before serving, toss salad with dressing.
8 (1½-cup) servings.

NUTRITION INFORMATION PER SERVING

Serving Size: 1½ cups		Percent U.S. RDA	
Calories	80	Protein	2%
Protein	2g	Vitamin A	50%
Carbohydrate	13g	Vitamin C	60%
Fat	4g	Thiamine	2%
Cholesterol	0mg	Riboflavin	6%
Sodium	30mg	Niacin	*
Potassium	260mg	Calcium	4%
		Iron	6%
*Contains less than 2%			

Cheddar Potatoes with Wreath of Vegetables

1¼ cups water
2 tablespoons margarine or butter
⅛ teaspoon garlic powder
⅛ teaspoon pepper
2½ cups mashed potato flakes
1 cup milk
4 ounces (1 cup) shredded Cheddar cheese
2 teaspoons prepared mustard
2 eggs, slightly beaten
1 (16-ounce) package frozen broccoli, cauliflower and carrots
2 tablespoons margarine or butter

Heat oven to 325°F. Lightly grease 2-quart casserole. In medium saucepan, bring water, 2 tablespoons margarine, garlic powder and pepper to a boil. Remove from heat; stir in potato flakes, milk, cheese, mustard and eggs until well blended. Place potato mixture in greased casserole. Using back of spoon, make indentation in potato mixture around edge of casserole 2 inches wide by 1 inch deep.* Bake at 325°F. for 20 to 25 minutes or until thoroughly heated.

Meanwhile, cook vegetables according to package directions; drain. Add 2 tablespoons margarine; stir to coat. Spoon cooked vegetables into indented ring in hot potato mixture.
8 servings.

TIP: *To make ahead, prepare potatoes to this point. Cover; refrigerate up to 24 hours. Bake at 325°F. for 30 to 35 minutes or until thoroughly heated. Continue as directed above.

NUTRITION INFORMATION PER SERVING

Serving Size: ⅛ of recipe		Percent U.S. RDA	
		Protein	10%
Calories	220	Vitamin A	40%
Protein	9g	Vitamin C	25%
Carbohydrate	19g	Thiamine	2%
Fat	13g	Riboflavin	10%
Cholesterol	70mg	Niacin	6%
Sodium	250mg	Calcium	20%
Potassium	330mg	Iron	4%

Pictured clockwise from top: Cheddar Potatoes with Wreath of Vegetables; Beef Rib Roast; Jicama Spinach Salad

Beef Rib Roast

4 to 6-pound standing beef rib roast
Salt and pepper

Heat oven to 325°F. Sprinkle roast with salt and pepper. Place, fat side up, on rack in shallow roasting pan. Insert meat thermometer so bulb reaches center of thickest part of meat but does not rest in fat or on bone. Roast at 325°F. for 2 to 4 hours or until desired degree of doneness.* For ease in carving, let roast stand 15 minutes to set juices.

8 to 12 servings.

TIP: *Roast to 140°F. for rare meat, 160°F. for medium meat and 170°F. for well-done meat.

NUTRITION INFORMATION PER SERVING

Serving Size: 1/12 of recipe		Percent U.S. RDA	
Calories	250	Protein	45%
Protein	28g	Vitamin A	*
Carbohydrate	0g	Vitamin C	*
Fat	14g	Thiamine	6%
Cholesterol	85mg	Riboflavin	10%
Sodium	170mg	Niacin	20%
Potassium	390mg	Calcium	*
		Iron	15%
*Contains less than 2%			

Horseradish Sauce

½ cup whipping cream
¼ teaspoon salt
¼ teaspoon dry mustard
Dash white pepper
3 tablespoons prepared horseradish

In small bowl, beat whipping cream, salt, dry mustard and pepper until soft peaks form. Fold in horseradish. Store covered in refrigerator.

1 cup.

NUTRITION INFORMATION PER SERVING

Serving Size: 1 tablespoon		Percent U.S. RDA	
		Protein	*
Calories	25	Vitamin A	2%
Protein	0g	Vitamin C	*
Carbohydrate	1g	Thiamine	*
Fat	3g	Riboflavin	*
Cholesterol	10mg	Niacin	*
Sodium	35mg	Calcium	*
Potassium	15mg	Iron	*
		*Contains less than 2%	

Jicama Spinach Salad

Pomegranates are available only around the holiday season, so enjoy them while you can! To use them, peel the skin away; loosen and separate the red seeds from the membranes.

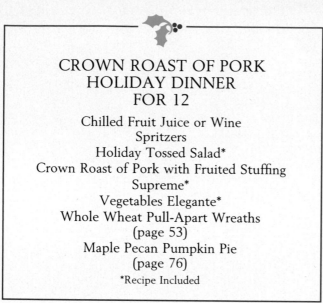

CROWN ROAST OF PORK HOLIDAY DINNER FOR 12

Chilled Fruit Juice or Wine
Spritzers
Holiday Tossed Salad*
Crown Roast of Pork with Fruited Stuffing
Supreme*
Vegetables Elegante*
Whole Wheat Pull-Apart Wreaths
(page 53)
Maple Pecan Pumpkin Pie
(page 76)
*Recipe Included

Holiday Tossed Salad

DRESSING
¼ cup olive oil
2 tablespoons honey
2 tablespoons white wine vinegar
1 small garlic clove, minced
¼ teaspoon freshly ground pepper
⅛ teaspoon salt
⅛ teaspoon dry mustard
¼ teaspoon grated lemon peel

SALAD
12 cups torn assorted salad greens

In small jar with tight-fitting lid, combine all dressing ingredients; shake well. Refrigerate several hours to blend flavors.

Place greens in large bowl. Just before serving, pour dressing over greens; toss lightly. Top with sliced tomato and grated lemon peel, if desired.
12 (1-cup) servings.

NUTRITION INFORMATION PER SERVING

Serving Size: 1 cup		Percent U.S. RDA	
Calories	60	Protein	*
Protein	1g	Vitamin A	15%
Carbohydrate	4g	Vitamin C	10%
Fat	5g	Thiamine	2%
Cholesterol	0mg	Riboflavin	2%
Sodium	25mg	Niacin	*
Potassium	135mg	Calcium	2%
		Iron	2%
		*Contains less than 2%	

Crown Roast of Pork with Fruited Stuffing Supreme

1 (9-pound) pork crown roast*
Salt and pepper

STUFFING
¼ cup margarine or butter
2 cups chopped celery
¾ cup chopped onions
1 cup chicken broth
1 teaspoon sage leaves, crushed
1 teaspoon poultry seasoning
16 ounces (6½ cups) unseasoned
   stuffing cubes
1 pound pork sausage, browned,
   well drained
1 (8-ounce) can crushed pineapple,
   undrained
1 cup applesauce
1 cup orange marmalade

Heat oven to 325°F. Sprinkle roast with salt and pepper, if desired. Place in roasting pan, bone tips up. Wrap tips of bones with foil to prevent excessive browning. Insert meat thermometer so bulb reaches center of thickest part of meat but does not rest in fat or on bone. (Do not add water; do not cover.) Roast on lowest oven rack at 325°F. for 2 hours.

Meanwhile, melt margarine in large skillet. Add celery and onions; cook about 5 minutes or until vegetables are crisp-tender, stirring constantly. Stir in broth, sage leaves and poultry seasoning. In very large bowl, combine stuffing cubes, sausage, pineapple, applesauce and marmalade. Add vegetable mixture; stir until well blended. Fill center of roast with stuffing; continue roasting until meat thermometer reaches 160°F. and stuffing is thoroughly heated. Cover stuffing with foil if top becomes too brown. (Remaining stuffing can be baked in 1½-quart covered casserole.) To serve, remove foil from stuffing and rib ends. If desired, cover bone ends with paper frills. Carefully transfer roast to serving platter; remove strings. For ease in carving, let roast stand 10 minutes to set juices. Slice meat between ribs.
16 servings.

Pictured left to right: Crown Roast of Pork with Fruited Stuffing Supreme; Holiday Tossed Salad

TIP: *A 4-pound boneless pork loin roast can be substituted. Roast uncovered in roasting pan 2 to 2½ hours or until meat thermometer reaches 160°F. Prepare stuffing as directed above and bake in covered casserole.

NUTRITION INFORMATION PER SERVING

Serving Size: ⅟₁₆ of recipe		Percent U.S. RDA	
		Protein	60%
Calories	470	Vitamin A	4%
Protein	39g	Vitamin C	6%
Carbohydrate	23g	Thiamine	60%
Fat	24g	Riboflavin	25%
Cholesterol	109mg	Niacin	40%
Sodium	360mg	Calcium	4%
Potassium	680mg	Iron	10%

Vegetables Elegante

2 (16-ounce) packages frozen broccoli, cauliflower and carrots
½ cup sliced green onions
2 (4.5-ounce) jars sliced mushrooms, drained
¼ cup margarine or butter
1 teaspoon celery salt

Cook vegetables with onions according to package directions; drain. Stir in remaining ingredients; heat thoroughly.
12 (⅔-cup) servings.

NUTRITION INFORMATION PER SERVING

Serving Size: ⅔ cup		Percent U.S. RDA	
Calories	60	Protein	2%
Protein	2g	Vitamin A	40%
Carbohydrate	6g	Vitamin C	35%
Fat	4g	Thiamine	2%
Cholesterol	0mg	Riboflavin	2%
Sodium	270mg	Niacin	4%
Potassium	180mg	Calcium	2%
		Iron	2%

Vegetable Beef Soup with Wild Rice

3 pounds beef ribs
1 tablespoon oil
8 cups water
2 teaspoons salt
¼ to ½ teaspoon cayenne pepper
1 bay leaf
1 cup sliced carrots
½ cup uncooked wild rice, rinsed
½ cup chopped onion
1 tablespoon Worcestershire sauce
1 to 2 garlic cloves, minced
1 (28-ounce) can (3 cups) tomatoes, cut up
½ cup sliced celery
1 medium green bell pepper, chopped
Hot pepper sauce, if desired

In Dutch oven, brown beef ribs in oil. Add water, salt, cayenne pepper and bay leaf. Bring to a boil. Reduce heat; cover and simmer 1½ to 2 hours or until meat is tender. Remove meat and bay leaf from broth; cool.

Skim fat from broth. Stir in carrots, wild rice, onion, Worcestershire sauce, garlic and tomatoes. Bring to a boil. Reduce heat; cover and simmer 30 minutes. Meanwhile, remove meat from bones; cut into bite-sized pieces. Stir in meat, celery and green pepper. Cover and simmer an additional 30 minutes or until vegetables and rice are tender.

Pass hot pepper sauce to be added to individual servings as desired.

8 (1½-cup) servings.

NUTRITION INFORMATION PER SERVING

Serving Size: 1½ cups		Percent U.S. RDA	
Calories	260	Protein	35%
Protein	22g	Vitamin A	100%
Carbohydrate	16g	Vitamin C	30%
Fat	12g	Thiamine	8%
Cholesterol	57mg	Riboflavin	10%
Sodium	780mg	Niacin	25%
Potassium	630mg	Calcium	4%
		Iron	15%

Oyster Stew

3 cups milk
3 cups half-and-half
½ cup margarine or butter
4½ cups shucked fresh oysters, undrained*
⅓ cup finely chopped onion
1 to 2 tablespoons chopped fresh parsley
1 to 2 tablespoons chopped pimiento
1½ teaspoons salt
¾ teaspoon pepper
¼ teaspoon Worcestershire sauce
Oyster crackers, if desired

In Dutch oven, combine milk and half-and-half; heat slowly until tiny bubbles appear around edges.

Melt margarine in large saucepan. Add oysters and onion. Cook over low heat 8 to 10 minutes or until edges of oysters begin to curl. Add oyster mixture, parsley, pimiento, salt, pepper and Worcestershire sauce to hot milk mixture. Heat gently, stirring frequently. *Do not boil.* Garnish each serving with oyster crackers.

8 (1½-cup) servings.

TIP: *Four or five 8-ounce cans oysters, undrained, can be substituted for fresh oysters. Reduce salt to ½ teaspoon. Cook margarine, oyster and onion mixture over low heat 4 to 6 minutes or until edges of oysters begin to curl.

NUTRITION INFORMATION PER SERVING

Serving Size: 1½ cups		Percent U.S. RDA	
Calories	380	Protein	25%
Protein	16g	Vitamin A	30%
Carbohydrate	18g	Vitamin C	15%
Fat	28g	Thiamine	20%
Cholesterol	117mg	Riboflavin	30%
Sodium	820mg	Niacin	10%
Potassium	610mg	Calcium	30%
		Iron	50%

Oyster Stew

Creamy Broccoli Leek Soup

8 cups chicken broth
2 pounds fresh broccoli, washed,
  cup into florets and ½-inch stem
  pieces (10 cups)
4 leeks
⅓ cup margarine or butter
⅓ cup flour
¼ to ½ teaspoon mace or nutmeg
¼ to ½ teaspoon pepper
2 cups half-and-half
5 ounces (1¼ cups) shredded
  Jarlsberg cheese
  Broccoli florets, if desired

In Dutch oven, bring chicken broth to a boil. Add 2 pounds broccoli; simmer uncovered 15 minutes or until tender. Meanwhile, cut green tops off leeks; discard tops. Cut leeks in half lengthwise; cut halves into thin slices.

Using slotted spoon, remove broccoli from broth. Reserve 1½ cups hot broth. In blender container or food processor bowl with metal blade, puree half of cooked broccoli and ¾ cup reserved hot broth until very smooth. Reserve 2 cups puree; set aside. Pour remaining puree into Dutch oven. Puree remaining broccoli with remaining ¾ cup hot broth; pour into Dutch oven.

In large skillet, cook leeks in margarine about 5 minutes or until tender, stirring occasionally. Stir in flour, mace and pepper; cook 1 minute, stirring constantly. Stir in 2 cups broccoli puree; blend well. Add to puree in Dutch oven; blend well. Bring to a boil over medium heat; cook 3 to 4 minutes or until soup is thickened, stirring constantly. Reduce heat to low; add half-and-half and cheese. Cook until cheese is melted, stirring frequently. *Do not boil.* Garnish with broccoli florets.
8 (1½-cup) servings.

NUTRITION INFORMATION PER SERVING

Serving Size: 1½ cups		Percent U.S. RDA	
Calories	350	Protein	25%
Protein	17g	Vitamin A	50%
Carbohydrate	24g	Vitamin C	150%
Fat	22g	Thiamine	10%
Cholesterol	39mg	Riboflavin	25%
Sodium	980mg	Niacin	25%
Potassium	850mg	Calcium	35%
		Iron	20%

Creamy Broccoli Leek Soup

Mace is a ground spice made from the dried outer covering of the nutmeg seed. It delicately enhances the flavor of this creamy soup.

```
┌─────────────────────────────────────┐
│                                     │
│   COMPANY'S COMING OPEN HOUSE       │
│            FOR 20                   │
│                                     │
│       Rosy Mulled Punches*          │
│       Cheesy Pita Canapés*          │
│       Crab Cheese Fondue*           │
│       French-Bread Cubes            │
│  Sweet 'n Sour Ham and Pineapple    │
│              Bites*                 │
│     Cocktail Sandwich Wreath*       │
│       Herbed Vegetable Dip*         │
│   Assorted Cut-Up Fresh Vegetables  │
│  Onion Jam and Cream Cheese Spread* │
│     Assorted Crackers and Thinly    │
│      Sliced Snack Rye Bread         │
│   Savory Spiced Nuts (page 129)     │
│                or                   │
│     Candied Pecans (page 43)        │
│    Apricot-Raisin Brandy Balls      │
│             (page 38)               │
│  Easy Chocolate Truffles (page 39)  │
│     Assorted Cookies made from      │
│    Holiday Cookie Mix (page 8)      │
│          *Recipe Included           │
│                                     │
└─────────────────────────────────────┘
```

Rosy Mulled Punches

SYRUP
  2 cups water
  1 cup sugar
  1 teaspoon whole cloves
  1 teaspoon whole allspice
  2 cinnamon sticks
  1 lemon, sliced
  1 orange, sliced

NONALCOHOLIC PUNCH
  1½ quarts (6 cups) raspberry-
    cranberry drink

ALCOHOLIC PUNCH
  2 (750 ml) bottles (6 cups) dry red
    wine

In small saucepan, combine all syrup ingredients. Cook over medium heat until mixture comes to a boil, stirring constantly. Reduce heat; simmer 10 minutes. Strain and cool. Refrigerate syrup until serving time.

At serving time, place half of prepared syrup (about 1¼ cups) in each of 2 large saucepans. To one add raspberry-cranberry drink. To the other add wine. Simmer each over low heat until thoroughly heated. Serve hot with cinnamon sticks and citrus twists, if desired. **14 (½-cup) servings of Nonalcoholic Punch and 14 (½-cup) servings of Alcoholic Punch.**

NUTRITION INFORMATION: Variables in this recipe make it impossible to calculate nutrition information.

Cheesy Pita Canapés

  2 (6-inch) pocket breads
  ½ cup mayonnaise or salad dressing
  ½ teaspoon dill weed
  4 ounces (1 cup) shredded
    mozzarella cheese
  ½ cup sliced pimiento-stuffed green
    olives
  3 tablespoons chopped green
    onions

Split pocket breads into 4 rounds. Place on ungreased cookie sheet. Broil 4 to 6 inches from heat for 1 to 2 minutes or until lightly toasted. In small bowl, combine mayonnaise and dill; mix well. Spread mixture on toasted rounds. Top each with cheese, olives and onions. Broil 2 to 3 minutes or until cheese is melted. Cut each round into 6 wedges. Serve immediately. **24 canapés.**

NUTRITION INFORMATION PER SERVING

Serving Size: 1 Canapé		Percent U.S. RDA	
Calories	70	Protein	2%
Protein	2g	Vitamin A	4%
Carbohydrate	4g	Vitamin C	*
Fat	5g	Thiamine	*
Cholesterol	3mg	Riboflavin	*
Sodium	135mg	Niacin	*
Potassium	10mg	Calcium	4%
		Iron	*
*Contains less than 2%			

Pictured left to right: Cocktail Sandwich Wreath; Rosy Mulled Punches; Sweet 'n Sour Ham and Pineapple Bites, page 114

Cocktail Sandwich Wreath

    3 cups cubed cooked chicken
 ½ cup chopped celery
 ½ cup chopped red apple
 ⅔ cup mayonnaise or salad dressing
    4 teaspoons lemon juice
 ½ teaspoon salt
    Dash white pepper
    Margarine or butter, softened
   40 slices rye or pumpernickel
       cocktail bread
    Leaf lettuce

In food processor bowl with metal blade, process chicken, celery, apple, mayonnaise, lemon juice, salt and pepper until small pieces of chicken, celery and apple remain.* Spread margarine on 1 side of each slice of bread. Spread 2 heaping teaspoons chicken mixture on each slice. Top with small piece of lettuce. Arrange open-faced sandwiches, slightly overlapping, on large platter to form wreath shape.** Garnish as desired.

40 open-faced sandwiches.

TIPS: *If desired, chicken, celery and apple can be finely chopped with knife. In medium bowl, mix chopped ingredients with mayonnaise, lemon juice, salt and pepper until well blended.

**Wreath can be prepared several hours before serving. Wrap tightly with plastic wrap and refrigerate until serving time.

NUTRITION INFORMATION PER SERVING

Serving Size: 1 sandwich		Percent U.S. RDA	
Calories	70	Protein	6%
Protein	4g	Vitamin A	*
Carbohydrate	4g	Vitamin C	*
Fat	5g	Thiamine	*
Cholesterol	12mg	Riboflavin	2%
Sodium	110mg	Niacin	6%
Potassium	50mg	Calcium	*
		Iron	*
		*Contains less than 2%	

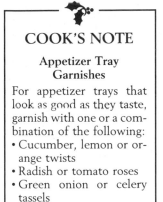

COOK'S NOTE

Appetizer Tray Garnishes

For appetizer trays that look as good as they taste, garnish with one or a combination of the following:
• Cucumber, lemon or orange twists
• Radish or tomato roses
• Green onion or celery tassels
• Cucumber or carrot curls
• Sprigs of parsley or mint

Crab Cheese Fondue

1 pound American cheese, cubed
¼ cup milk
2 tablespoons margarine or butter
1 (6-ounce) package frozen crab meat, thawed, drained, chopped
¼ cup dry sherry
2 tablespoons chopped pimiento
Dash garlic powder

In top of double boiler, combine American cheese, milk and margarine. Cook over hot water until cheese is melted, stirring constantly. Stir in crab, sherry, pimiento and garlic powder; heat thoroughly. Serve with French-bread cubes.
3 cups.

MICROWAVE DIRECTIONS: In medium-sized microwave-safe bowl, combine cheese, milk and margarine. Microwave on MEDIUM for 5 to 8 minutes or until cheese is melted, stirring every 2 minutes. Stir in crab, sherry, pimiento and garlic powder; mix well. Microwave on MEDIUM for 2 to 3 minutes or until hot; stir before serving. Serve with French-bread cubes.

NUTRITION INFORMATION PER SERVING

Serving Size: 1 tablespoon		Percent U.S. RDA	
Calories	45	Protein	4%
Protein	3g	Vitamin A	2%
Carbohydrate	0g	Vitamin C	*
Fat	4g	Thiamine	*
Cholesterol	11mg	Riboflavin	2%
Sodium	180mg	Niacin	*
Potassium	30mg	Calcium	6%
		Iron	*
*Contains less than 2%			

Sweet 'n Sour Ham and Pineapple Bites

1 (20-ounce) can pineapple chunks in heavy syrup, drained (reserving syrup)
3 tablespoons brown sugar
1 tablespoon cornstarch
¼ cup cider vinegar
2 tablespoons orange juice
2 cups cubed cooked ham
1 cup cocktail-size cooked sausage links
1 small green or red bell pepper, cut into 1-inch pieces

Measure pineapple syrup; add water if necessary to equal ⅔ cup. In small saucepan, combine pineapple liquid, brown sugar, cornstarch, vinegar and orange juice. Cook over medium heat until mixture boils and thickens, stirring constantly. Add pineapple chunks, ham and sausage; cook until thoroughly heated. Stir in green pepper. Immediately place in chafing dish or fondue pot. Serve with decorative toothpicks.
5 cups.

MICROWAVE DIRECTIONS: Measure ½ *cup pineapple syrup.* In 2½-quart microwave-safe bowl or 8-cup microwave-safe measuring cup, combine pineapple liquid, brown sugar, cornstarch, vinegar and orange juice. Microwave on HIGH for 4 to 5 minutes or until sauce is thickened, stirring once. Stir in pineapple chunks, ham and sausage. Microwave on HIGH for 4 to 5 minutes or until mixture is thoroughly heated, stirring once. Continue as directed above.

NUTRITION INFORMATION PER SERVING

Serving Size: ¼ cup		Percent U.S. RDA	
Calories	80	Protein	6%
Protein	4g	Vitamin A	*
Carbohydrate	9g	Vitamin C	10%
Fat	3g	Thiamine	8%
Cholesterol	12mg	Riboflavin	2%
Sodium	250mg	Niacin	2%
Potassium	100mg	Calcium	*
		Iron	2%
*Contains less than 2%			

COOK'S NOTE

Open House Hints

Planning is the main ingredient of a successful gathering, formal or informal, large or small. Advance planning means more time for shopping, preparing foods, readying your home and other creative touches.

• Use our menu or plan a menu in keeping with the occasion and your budget, timetable, culinary skills and preferences. Consider the number of guests, oven capacity, refrigerator and freezer space, and other supplies like serving dishes. Be realistic about what you can handle with ease.

• For buffet service, foods should be easy to serve and eat.

• Foods that can be partially made ahead help keep party-day preparations to a minimum.

• Use checklists to keep track of things to do and when to do them, such as buying groceries, preparing foods and getting the house ready with linens, tableware, tables and chairs.

Onion Jam

¼ cup oil
½ cup sugar
4 cups coarsely chopped Bermuda
  or Spanish onions
¼ teaspoon salt
  Dash pepper
½ cup red wine vinegar
½ teaspoon caraway seed

Heat oil in large skillet over medium heat. Add sugar; cook, stirring constantly, until mixture becomes a light caramel color, about 10 minutes. Add onions, salt and pepper; cook 15 minutes over medium heat, stirring frequently. Add vinegar and caraway seed; simmer 30 minutes. Remove from heat. Ladle into clean container; cool completely. Store in refrigerator up to 3 weeks. Serve as a spread with crackers, cocktail bread or melba rounds or use to prepare Onion Jam and Cream Cheese Spread.
1½ cups.

NUTRITION INFORMATION PER SERVING

Serving Size: 1 tablespoon		Percent U.S. RDA	
		Protein	*
Calories	45	Vitamin A	*
Protein	0g	Vitamin C	*
Carbohydrate	6g	Thiamine	*
Fat	2g	Riboflavin	*
Cholesterol	0mg	Niacin	*
Sodium	20mg	Calcium	*
Potassium	45mg	Iron	*
		*Contains less than 2%	

Onion Jam and Cream Cheese Spread

1 (8-ounce package) cream cheese,
  softened
1 cup Onion Jam

Place cream cheese on serving plate. Top cheese with Onion Jam. Serve with assorted crackers and thinly sliced snack rye bread.
2 cups.

NUTRITION INFORMATION PER SERVING

Serving Size: 1 tablespoon		Percent U.S. RDA	
		Protein	*
Calories	50	Vitamin A	2%
Protein	1g	Vitamin C	*
Carbohydrate	3g	Thiamine	*
Fat	4g	Riboflavin	*
Cholesterol	8mg	Niacin	*
Sodium	30mg	Calcium	*
Potassium	30mg	Iron	*
		*Contains less than 2%	

Herbed Vegetable Dip

1 (8-ounce) package cream cheese,
  softened
½ cup dairy sour cream
⅓ cup mayonnaise or salad dressing
⅓ cup chopped fresh parsley
1 tablespoon sliced green onions
2 teaspoons dill weed
¼ teaspoon garlic salt
2 teaspoons lemon juice
  Several drops hot pepper sauce

In food processor bowl with metal blade, combine all ingredients and process until thoroughly blended, stopping to scrape down sides of bowl once or twice.* Place in serving bowl; cover. Refrigerate several hours to blend flavors. Serve with assorted cut-up fresh vegetables.
2 cups.

TIP: *Ingredients can be combined in small bowl. Stir until thoroughly blended.

NUTRITION INFORMATION PER SERVING

Serving Size: 1 tablespoon		Percent U.S. RDA	
		Protein	*
Calories	50	Vitamin A	2%
Protein	1g	Vitamin C	*
Carbohydrate	1g	Thiamine	*
Fat	5g	Riboflavin	*
Cholesterol	11mg	Niacin	*
Sodium	50mg	Calcium	*
Potassium	20mg	Iron	*
		*Contains less than 2%	

Onion Jam and Cream Cheese Spread

Remember green pepper jelly served over cream cheese? Our newest spin-off features Onion Jam. Our taste panel members loved it and we hope you will too!

Herbed Vegetable Dip

A good recipe to prepare early in the day or even the day before your party to allow for full flavor development.

Sparkling Brunch Punch

ICE RING
1 (10-ounce) package frozen
  raspberries, thawed, drained
  (reserving syrup)
Lemon slices
Lime slices

PUNCH
2 (25.4-ounce) bottles sparkling
  white grape juice, chilled
1 (28-ounce) bottle club soda,
  chilled
1 (12-ounce) can frozen pink
  lemonade concentrate, thawed

To prepare ice ring, arrange drained raspberries, lemon slices and lime slices in an attractive design in 5-cup ring mold. Pour water into mold to partially cover berries and slices; freeze until firm. Fill water to within ½ inch of top of mold; freeze completely.

Prepare punch just before serving. In punch bowl, combine reserved raspberry syrup, sparkling grape juice, club soda and lemonade concentrate; stir gently to blend. Unmold ice ring and float, fruit side up, in punch bowl.
24 (½-cup) servings.

NUTRITION INFORMATION PER SERVING

Serving Size: ½ cup		Percent U.S. RDA	
Calories	70	Protein	*
Protein	0g	Vitamin A	*
Carbohydrate	19g	Vitamin C	4%
Fat	0g	Thiamine	*
Cholesterol	0mg	Riboflavin	2%
Sodium	10mg	Niacin	*
Potassium	100mg	Calcium	*
		Iron	*

*Contains less than 2%

Make-Ahead Eggnog French Toast

6 eggs
2 cups half-and-half or milk
¼ cup sugar
¼ teaspoon nutmeg
1½ teaspoons vanilla
¾ teaspoon rum extract
16 to 18 slices firm white or whole
  wheat bread
  Butter or margarine, melted
  Powdered sugar, if desired

Grease 2 cookie sheets. In medium bowl, combine eggs, half-and-half, sugar, nutmeg, vanilla and rum extract; beat until well blended. Dip each slice of bread in egg mixture; place on greased cookie sheets. Cover lightly with foil; freeze 1 to 2 hours or until completely frozen. To store, remove from freezer; stack slices, placing waxed paper between, and wrap stack in foil. Return to freezer.

Heat oven to 425°F. Remove bread slices from freezer; brush 1 side with melted butter. Place buttered side down on ungreased cookie sheets. Bake at 425°F. for 10 minutes. Brush top with butter; turn buttered side down. Return to oven and bake an additional 10 to 15 minutes or until golden brown. Sprinkle with powdered sugar.
16 to 18 slices.

NUTRITION INFORMATION PER SERVING

Serving Size: 1 slice		Percent U.S. RDA	
Calories	180	Protein	8%
Protein	5g	Vitamin A	6%
Carbohydrate	18g	Vitamin C	*
Fat	9g	Thiamine	8%
Cholesterol	90mg	Riboflavin	10%
Sodium	210mg	Niacin	4%
Potassium	85mg	Calcium	6%
		Iron	6%

*Contains less than 2%

Pictured clockwise from top: Maple-Glazed Sausages; Tart 'n Tangy Fruit Compote; Make-Ahead Eggnog French Toast

Tart 'n Tangy Fruit Compote

1 (6-ounce) can frozen orange-
   pineapple juice concentrate,
   thawed
¼ teaspoon cinnamon
1 teaspoon brandy extract or
   1 tablespoon brandy
1 (11-ounce) can mandarin orange
   segments, drained
1 (8-ounce) can pineapple chunks
   in their own juice, undrained
1 cup seedless red or purple grapes
1 large tart green apple, unpeeled,
   cubed

In large bowl, combine juice concentrate, cinnamon and brandy extract;
blend well. Add fruits; toss gently. Refrigerate at least 1 hour to blend flavors.
Stir gently before serving.
6 (½ cup) servings.

NUTRITION INFORMATION PER SERVING

Serving Size: ½ cup		Percent U.S. RDA	
Calories	140	Protein	*
Protein	1g	Vitamin A	8%
Carbohydrate	35g	Vitamin C	70%
Fat	0g	Thiamine	10%
Cholesterol	0mg	Riboflavin	2%
Sodium	0mg	Niacin	2%
Potassium	370mg	Calcium	2%
		Iron	2%
		*Contains less than 2%	

Maple-Glazed Sausages

2 (8-ounce) packages brown 'n
   serve sausage links
1 cup maple-flavored syrup
½ cup firmly packed brown sugar
1 teaspoon cinnamon

In large skillet, brown sausage links;
drain. In small bowl, combine syrup,
brown sugar and cinnamon; blend well.
Pour over sausages. Heat thoroughly
until sausages are well coated, stirring
gently.
6 to 8 servings.

NUTRITION INFORMATION PER SERVING

Serving Size: ⅛ of		Percent U.S. RDA	
recipe		Protein	8%
Calories	250	Vitamin A	*
Protein	5g	Vitamin C	*
Carbohydrate	39g	Thiamine	10%
Fat	8g	Riboflavin	4%
Cholesterol	22mg	Niacin	6%
Sodium	350mg	Calcium	2%
Potassium	160mg	Iron	4%
		*Contains less than 2%	

Maple-Glazed Sausages

*If desired, spoon the thick sweet
sauce over Make-Ahead Eggnog French Toast.*

MERRY AND BRIGHT BRUNCH
FOR 12

Cran-Raspberry Sparkle*
Brunch Egg Bake*
Holiday Coffee Braid*
or
Partridge Bread with Orange-
Honey Butter (page 46)
Assorted Cut-Up Fresh Fruit
Coffee or Tea
*Recipe Included

Holiday Coffee Braid

6½ to 7½ cups all purpose or
    unbleached flour
1 cup sugar
2 teaspoons salt
1 teaspoon freshly crushed
    cardamom
2 packages active dry yeast
1½ cups milk
½ cup water
½ cup margarine or butter
2 eggs
1 egg, slightly beaten
½ cup sliced almonds
¼ cup pearl sugar or crushed sugar
    cubes

Lightly grease 2 cookie sheets. Lightly spoon flour into measuring cup; level off. In large bowl, combine 3 cups flour, sugar, salt, cardamom and yeast; blend well. In medium saucepan, heat milk, water and margarine until very warm (120 to 130°F.). Add warm liquid and 2 eggs to flour mixture. Blend at low speed until moistened; beat 3 minutes at medium speed. By hand, stir in an additional 3 to 3½ cups flour until dough pulls away from sides of bowl. On floured surface, knead in remaining ½ to 1 cup flour until dough is smooth and elastic, about 5 minutes. Place dough in greased bowl; cover loosely with plastic wrap and cloth towel. Let rise in warm place (80 to 85°F.) until light and doubled in size, about 1½ hours.

Punch down dough several times to remove all air bubbles. Divide dough in half; divide one half into 3 pieces. Shape each piece into 18-inch rope; place on greased cookie sheet. Braid 3 ropes loosely from center to each end. Pinch ends together; tuck under to seal. Repeat with remaining dough; cover. Let rise in warm place 30 to 40 minutes or until almost doubled in size.

Heat oven to 375°F. Brush braids with beaten egg; sprinkle with almonds and pearl sugar. Bake at 375°F. for 25 to 35 minutes or until golden brown. Remove from cookie sheets; cool on wire racks.
2 (16-slice) loaves.

HIGH ALTITUDE – Above 3500 Feet: No change.

NUTRITION INFORMATION PER SERVING

Serving Size: 1 slice		Percent U.S. RDA	
Calories	180	Protein	6%
Protein	4g	Vitamin A	2%
Carbohydrate	31g	Vitamin C	*
Fat	5g	Thiamine	15%
Cholesterol	21mg	Riboflavin	10%
Sodium	180mg	Niacin	10%
Potassium	75mg	Calcium	2%
		Iron	8%
*Contains less than 2%			

Cran-Raspberry Sparkle

4 cups raspberry-cranberry drink,
    chilled
1 (1-liter) bottle (4 cups) lemon-
    lime flavored carbonated
    beverage, chilled

Just before serving, combine raspberry-cranberry drink and carbonated beverage in 2-quart pitcher. Stir gently.
16 (½-cup) servings.

NUTRITION INFORMATION PER SERVING

Serving Size: ½ cup		Percent U.S. RDA	
Calories	60	Protein	*
Protein	0g	Vitamin A	*
Carbohydrate	16g	Vitamin C	35%
Fat	0g	Thiamine	*
Cholesterol	0mg	Riboflavin	*
Sodium	10mg	Niacin	*
Potassium	10mg	Calcium	*
		Iron	*
*Contains less than 2%			

Brunch Egg Bake

Brunch Egg Bake

12 ounces (3 cups) shredded
  Cheddar cheese
12 ounces (3 cups) shredded
  mozzarella cheese
1 (4.5-ounce) jar sliced
  mushrooms, drained
⅓ cup sliced green onions
½ medium red bell pepper,
  chopped
¼ cup margarine or butter, melted
8 ounces cooked ham, cut into thin
  julienne strips
½ cup all purpose or unbleached
  flour
1¾ cups milk
2 tablespoons chopped fresh
  parsley
8 eggs, beaten

In large bowl, combine cheeses. Sprinkle half of cheese mixture in ungreased 13 × 9-inch (3-quart) baking dish. In medium skillet, cook mushrooms, green onions and red bell pepper in margarine until onions and pepper are tender. Arrange vegetables over cheese. Arrange ham strips over vegetables. Sprinkle remaining cheese over ham.*

Heat oven to 350°F. Lightly spoon flour into measuring cup; level off. In large bowl, blend flour, milk, parsley and eggs; pour over layers in baking dish. Bake at 350°F. for 35 to 45 minutes or until mixture is set and top is lightly browned. Let stand 10 minutes; cut into squares. Garnish with red bell pepper and fresh parsley, if desired.

12 servings.

TIP: *To make ahead, prepare to this point; cover and refrigerate. Bake as directed above.

NUTRITION INFORMATION PER SERVING

Serving Size: ¹/₁₂ of recipe		Percent U.S. RDA	
Calories	340	Protein	40%
Protein	25g	Vitamin A	25%
Carbohydrate	8g	Vitamin C	10%
Fat	23g	Thiamine	15%
Cholesterol	199mg	Riboflavin	30%
Sodium	680mg	Niacin	6%
Potassium	240mg	Calcium	50%
		Iron	8%

Brunch Egg Bake

This casserole is similar to many stratas, which are baked egg and cheese dishes using layers of bread. In this recipe, cheese replaces the bread.

Homemade Gifts & Decorations

From Our Home to Yours

A knock at your neighbor's front door, a basket trimmed with ribbons and bows in hand. "Merry Christmas! Enjoy this on a cold December night!" you say and head on your way. Tucked in the folds of a red-and-white-checked dishcloth are a jar of Quick Spaghetti Sauce, a bottle of Spiced Vinegar Salad Dressing, a package of homemade spinach pasta, two candles and a bottle of red wine—all the fixings for a romantic Italian dinner. It will be one of the most memorable—and appreciated—gifts of the season.

Whether jars of jams, jellies or pickles made during the harvest days of late summer, a canister of versatile Holiday Muffin Mix or a tin of Savory Spiced Nuts perfect for entertaining, homemade gifts from your kitchen are gifts from the heart. They're reminiscent of simpler times and tastes. They can't be bought in any store or ordered over the phone. And they convey a sincerity in gift-giving that often gets overshadowed during the hustle and bustle of Christmas.

Give these food gifts singly, or combine them into theme baskets such as the fixings for an Italian dinner, breakfast in bed, a dessert sampler. For a special touch include items that can be used later, such as a cork-screw, two lovely wineglasses, a honey server, a tea infuser or a set of mugs. And the wrapping itself can be a gift—dishcloths, pretty napkins, place mats.

Besides gift ideas, you'll find directions for impressive yet easy decorations that you can make for your home. Festoon your tree with Tree Trimmer Cookie Houses and Tiny Twinklers, or fill your home with the spicy fragrance of Scented Cinnamon Ornaments and Scented Heart Wreaths.

Although this chapter focuses on gifts and decora-tions, remember to use the rest of the book for gift-giving ideas as well. You may want to give an as-sortment of candies and cookies with a cut-glass Christmas plate or wrap a loaf of savory bread with a cutting board and bread knife. Just give your imag-ination free rein.

Pictured clockwise from upper left: Apricot Double Dips; Chocolate Praline Ice Cream Topping; Flavored Mocha Mixes,
page 123

Apricot Double Dips

½ cup semi-sweet chocolate chips
2 tablespoons margarine or butter
1 (6-ounce) package dried apricots
½ cup vanilla milk chips

Line cookie sheets with waxed paper. In small saucepan over low heat, melt chocolate chips and margarine; stir until smooth. Remove from heat. Set saucepan in hot water to maintain dipping consistency. Dip 1 end of each apricot in chocolate mixture. Place on waxed paper-lined cookie sheets. Refrigerate until set.

Meanwhile, in small saucepan over low heat melt vanilla milk chips; stir until smooth. Set saucepan in hot water to maintain dipping consistency. Dip coated end of each apricot in melted vanilla chips to within ¼ inch of top edge of chocolate coating. Place on lined cookie sheets. Refrigerate until set. Place in paper candy cups. Cover; store in cool, dry place.
About 3½ dozen candies.

MICROWAVE DIRECTIONS: In 4-cup microwave-safe measuring cup, combine chocolate chips and margarine. Microwave on HIGH for 45 to 60 seconds or until melted; stir until smooth. Continue as directed above. In 4-cup microwave-safe measuring cup, place vanilla milk chips. Microwave on HIGH for 45 to 60 seconds or until melted; stir until smooth. Continue as directed above.

NUTRITION INFORMATION PER SERVING

Serving Size: 1 candy		Percent U.S. RDA	
Calories	35	Protein	*
Protein	0g	Vitamin A	6%
Carbohydrate	5g	Vitamin C	*
Fat	2g	Thiamine	*
Cholesterol	0mg	Riboflavin	*
Sodium	10mg	Niacin	*
Potassium	65mg	Calcium	*
		Iron	*
*Contains less than 2%			

Chocolate Praline Ice Cream Topping

⅔ cup firmly packed brown sugar
⅔ cup butter or margarine
1 cup whipping cream
1 (6-ounce) package (1 cup) semi-sweet chocolate chips
1 cup pecan halves

In medium saucepan, combine brown sugar, butter and whipping cream. Bring to a boil over medium heat, stirring constantly. Reduce heat; simmer 2 minutes, stirring occasionally. Add chocolate chips; stir until melted and smooth. Stir in pecans. Serve warm over ice cream or dessert. Cover; store in refrigerator. **3 cups.**

MICROWAVE DIRECTIONS: In a 4-cup microwave-safe measuring cup, combine brown sugar, butter and whipping cream. Microwave on HIGH for 4 to 4½ minutes or until mixture comes to a full boil, stirring once halfway through cooking. Add chocolate chips; stir until melted and smooth. Stir in pecans.

NUTRITION INFORMATION PER SERVING

Serving Size: 2 tablespoons		Percent U.S. RDA	
		Protein	*
Calories	170	Vitamin A	6%
Protein	1g	Vitamin C	*
Carbohydrate	11g	Thiamine	*
Fat	14g	Riboflavin	*
Cholesterol	27mg	Niacin	*
Sodium	60mg	Calcium	*
Potassium	70mg	Iron	2%
*Contains less than 2%			

Apricot Double Dips

If desired, vary the dipping technique to make a variety of designs.

Chocolate Praline Ice Cream Topping

Include a jar of this superb topping with your gift of an ice cream maker, or tuck a jar into a gift basket for chocolate lovers.

Sugar Cookie Tree

Transform sugar cookie dough into a Christmas tree worthy of being a table centerpiece or a long-remembered gift!

Sugar Cookie Tree

COOKIES
- 1 cup sugar
- 1 cup margarine or butter, softened
- 1 (3-ounce) package cream cheese, softened
- 1 teaspoon vanilla
- 1 egg yolk
- 2¼ cups all purpose or unbleached flour
- ½ teaspoon salt

FROSTING
- 2 cups powdered sugar
- 4 to 5 tablespoons milk
- Green food color
- Decorator candies, as desired

FOR ASSEMBLING TREE
- 1 yard ribbon, 1 inch wide
- Round Styrofoam base, 1 inch thick and 6 inches in diameter, or as desired
- 1 (10-inch) bamboo skewer
- 16 ring-shaped hard candies
- Large gumdrop for top star, or other decoration, as desired
- Heavy cardboard

In large bowl, beat sugar, margarine and cream cheese until light and fluffy. Add vanilla and egg yolk; blend well. Lightly spoon flour into measuring cup; level off. Add flour and salt; mix well. Cover with plastic wrap; refrigerate 2 hours for easier handling.

Trace pattern pieces and mark center; cut from heavy paper or light cardboard. (Or use set of graduated star cookie cutters.*) Also cut stars from heavy cardboard to use as supports beneath all but the 3 smallest cookie stars. (Cut cardboard slightly smaller than the cookie it will support.) Mark center of stars. Set aside for assembly.

Heat oven to 375°F. Lightly grease 3 cookie sheets. On well-floured surface, roll dough ⅓ at a time to ¼-inch thickness. (Refrigerate remaining dough.) Place patterns on dough and cut around with sharp knife; remove pattern pieces. Or cut out stars with lightly floured cookie cutters. Place stars 1 inch apart on greased cookie sheets. Bake at 375°F. for 7 to 10 minutes or until light golden brown. With end of bamboo skewer, make ⅛-inch hole in exact center of each star, using pattern as guide. Cool larger stars on cookie sheets 2 to 3 minutes. Remove from cookie sheets; place on wire racks. Cool all stars 3 to 4 hours.

In medium bowl, combine all frosting ingredients except candies, adding enough milk for thin spreading consistency. Frost cooled stars; decorate with candies as desired. Let frosting set overnight before assembling tree.

To assemble tree, pin ribbon around edge of Styrofoam base. Insert bamboo skewer in center of base for trunk of tree. Place largest star cookie and cardboard support on skewer to rest on Styrofoam base; add 2 ring-shaped candies. Using a heavy cardboard star for stability underneath each of the next cookies, place cookies on skewer with 2 ring-shaped candies between each one, ending with smallest star on top. Roll out gumdrop to ¼-inch thickness; cut star shape using top star pattern. Top tree with gumdrop star or decorative star. **1 cookie tree.**

TIP: *This recipe was tested with a set of 9 graduated star-shaped cookie cutters, and the largest star was about 8 inches wide. Smaller cookie cutter sets can be used, but bake times and assembly directions will vary. Cookie cutter sets are available at kitchen specialty shops.

HIGH ALTITUDE—Above 3500 Feet: No change.

NUTRITION INFORMATION: Variables in this recipe make it impossible to calculate nutrition information.

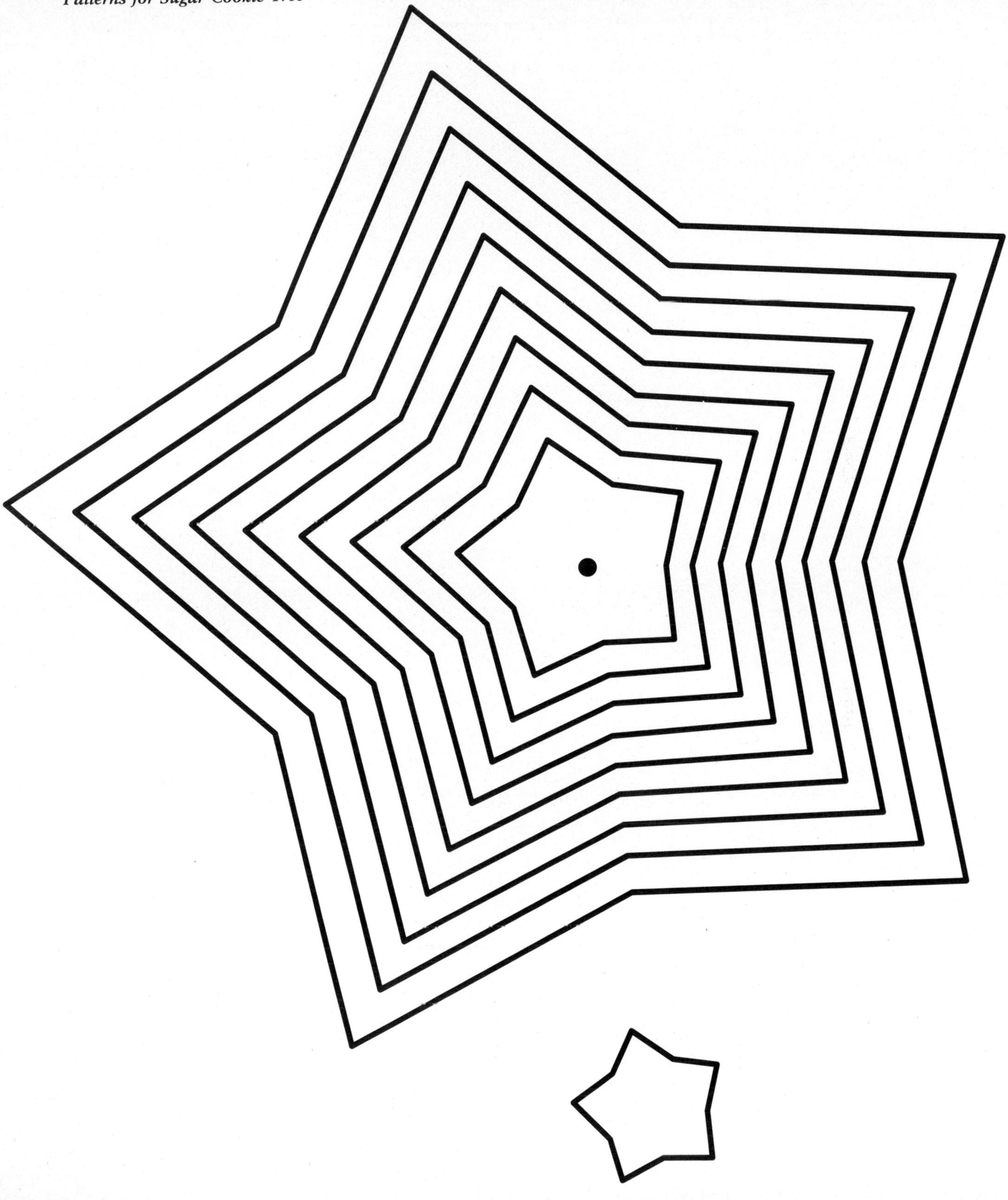

Scented Cinnamon Ornaments

Scented Cinnamon Ornaments

Scented Cinnamon Ornaments

Hang these inedible ornaments on the tree, tie them on holiday packages, or string a garland of them across the fireplace mantel. Supermarkets and food co-ops often sell these spices in bulk quantity.

1 (4-ounce) can (approximately 1 cup) cinnamon
1 tablespoon cloves
1 tablespoon nutmeg
¾ cup applesauce
2 tablespoons white glue
  Ribbon

In medium bowl, combine cinnamon, cloves and nutmeg. Add applesauce and glue; stir to combine. Work mixture with hands 2 to 3 minutes or until dough is smooth and ingredients are thoroughly mixed. Divide into 4 portions. On floured surface, roll each portion to ¼-inch thickness. Cut dough with floured cookie cutters of desired shapes. Using straw or toothpick, make a small hole in top of ornament. Place cutouts on wire racks and allow to dry at room temperature for several days.* Thread ribbon through hole in ornament. *Do not eat.*

About 32 (2-inch) ornaments.

TIP: *For a more uniform drying process, turn ornaments over once each day.

VARIATION:

SCENTED HEART WREATHS: Prepare Scented Cinnamon Ornaments recipe. Cut dough using heart-shaped cookie cutters. Dry cutouts as directed in recipe. Glue dried hearts onto wooden hoop, placing points of hearts toward center. Attach ribbon and decorate as desired.

Lemon-Mint Vinegar

4 sprigs fresh mint
1 lemon, peel removed in a spiral
  and cut in half
2 teaspoons lemon juice
4 cups white wine vinegar

In each of two 1-pint bottles, place 2 sprigs of mint. Add 1 spiral lemon peel and 1 teaspoon lemon juice to each. Fill bottles with white wine vinegar. Cork tightly; invert several times to blend ingredients. Let stand in cool, dark place for 3 weeks to develop flavor. Invert bottles occasionally. Use to make Lemon-Mint Salad Dressing.
2 pints.

Lemon-Mint Salad Dressing

In jar with tight-fitting lid, combine ½ cup oil, ½ cup Lemon-Mint Vinegar and 1 tablespoon sugar. Shake to blend. **1 cup.**

NUTRITION INFORMATION: Variables in this recipe make it impossible to calculate nutrition information.

Spiced Vinegar

2 cups sweet red wine
2 cups white vinegar
3 (3-inch) strips orange peel
2 (4-inch) cinnamon sticks
2 whole cloves

In medium saucepan, combine wine, vinegar, orange peel strips and cinnamon sticks. Bring to a boil; simmer 3 minutes. Strain into two 1-pint bottles. Add 1 strip orange peel, 1 cinnamon stick and 1 whole clove to each bottle. Cork tightly. Let stand in cool, dark place for 3 weeks to develop flavor. Invert bottles occasionally. Use to make Spiced Vinegar Salad Dressing. **2 pints.**

Spiced Vinegar Salad Dressing

In jar with tight-fitting lid, combine ½ cup oil, ½ cup Spiced Vinegar and 2 teaspoons sugar. Shake to blend. **1 cup.**

NUTRITION INFORMATION: Variables in this recipe make it impossible to calculate nutrition information.

Savory Spiced Nuts

2 tablespoons margarine or butter
½ teaspoon salt
2 tablespoons Worcestershire sauce
⅛ to ¼ teaspoon hot pepper sauce
  Dash garlic powder
⅔ cup whole almonds
⅔ cup pecan halves
⅔ cup whole hazelnuts (filberts)

Heat oven to 300°F. In medium saucepan over low heat, melt margarine. Stir in salt, Worcestershire sauce, hot pepper sauce and garlic powder. Add nuts; toss to coat. Spread nuts evenly in ungreased 15 × 10 × 1-inch baking pan. Bake at 300°F. for 30 to 35 minutes or until crisp and toasted, stirring occasionally. Cool completely. Store in airtight container.
2 cups.

MICROWAVE DIRECTIONS: In 4-cup microwave-safe measuring cup, microwave margarine on HIGH for 30 to 45 seconds or until melted. Stir in salt, Worcestershire sauce, hot pepper sauce and garlic powder. Add nuts; toss to coat. Spread nuts in 12 × 8-inch (2-quart) microwave-safe baking dish. Microwave on HIGH for 4 to 5 minutes or until nuts are toasted, stirring once every minute.

NUTRITION INFORMATION PER SERVING

Serving Size: ¼ cup		Percent U.S. RDA	
Calories	230	Protein	6%
Protein	5g	Vitamin A	2%
Carbohydrate	7g	Vitamin C	*
Fat	22g	Thiamine	6%
Cholesterol	0mg	Riboflavin	6%
Sodium	210mg	Niacin	2%
Potassium	170mg	Calcium	6%
		Iron	6%
*Contains less than 2%			

Lemon-Mint Vinegar

Make a flavorful homemade vinegar for a special friend who loves to cook. Pour it into a decorative bottle, attach the recipe for Lemon-Mint Salad Dressing and add a brightly colored bow.

Spiced Vinegar

A unique vinegar which makes a dressing that is ideal for salad greens and citrus fruit combinations.

Craft Gift Breads

Bake these inedible craft breads in any or all of the suggested shapes. Then follow the directions for preserving and decorating what is sure to be a special, long-lasting holiday gift.

5 to 6 cups all purpose or unbleached flour
3 tablespoons sugar
2 teaspoons salt
2 packages active dry yeast
2 cups water
¼ cup oil or shortening

(Craft Gift Breads are intended for decoration only; *do not eat.*)

Lightly spoon flour into measuring cup; level off. In large bowl, combine 2 cups flour, sugar, salt and yeast; blend well. In small saucepan, heat water and oil until very warm (120 to 130°F.). Add warm liquid to flour mixture. Blend at low speed until moistened; beat 3 minutes at medium speed. Stir in an additional 2½ to 3 cups flour until dough pulls cleanly away from sides of bowl. On floured surface, knead in remaining ½ to 1 cup flour until dough is smooth and elastic, about 5 minutes. Place dough in greased bowl; cover loosely with plastic wrap and cloth towel. Let rise in warm place until light and doubled in size, about 1 to 1¼ hours.

Punch down dough several times to remove all air bubbles. Follow shaping and baking directions for desired variation.

SHAPING AND BAKING VARIATIONS:

2 LARGE LOAVES: Grease two 8×4- or 9×5-inch loaf pans. Divide dough into 2 parts. Remove air pockets by working dough with hands. On lightly floured surface, roll each to 14×7-inch rectangle. Starting with shorter side, roll up; pinch edges firmly to seal. Place seam side down in greased pans. Cover; let rise in warm place until dough fills pans and tops of loaves are about 1 inch above pan edges, about 45 minutes. Heat oven to 375°F. Bake 45 to 55 minutes or until loaves sound hollow when lightly tapped. Immediately remove from pans; cool on wire racks.

6 MINI LOAVES AND 1 ROUND LOAF: Grease six 4×2-inch loaf pans and 1 cookie sheet. Divide dough into 10 parts. For 6 loaves, remove air pockets by working dough with hands. On lightly floured surface, roll each to 10×5-inch rectangle. Starting with shorter side, roll up; pinch edges firmly to seal. Place seam side down in greased pans. Cover; let rise in warm place until dough fills pans and tops of loaves are about ½ inch above pan edges, about 30 minutes. Combine 4 reserved parts; remove air pockets by working dough with hands. Shape into 1 round loaf. Place on greased cookie sheet. Cover; let rise in warm place until doubled in size, about 30 minutes. Heat oven to 375°F. Bake 25 to 35 minutes or until loaves sound hollow when lightly tapped. Immediately remove from pans and cookie sheet; cool on wire racks.

2 ROUND LOAVES: Grease 2 cookie sheets. Divide dough into 2 parts. Remove air pockets by working dough with hands; shape each into a round ball. Place on greased cookie sheets. Cover; let rise in warm place until doubled in size, about 30 minutes. If desired, with knife slash a ¼-inch-deep lattice design on top of loaves. Heat oven to 375°F. Bake 25 to 35 minutes or until loaves sound hollow when lightly tapped. Immediately remove from cookie sheets; cool on wire racks.

2 BRAIDS: Grease 2 cookie sheets. Divide dough into 2 parts. Remove air pockets by working dough with hands. On lightly floured surface, roll each to 12×9-inch rectangle. Cut each rectangle lengthwise into three 12×3-inch strips. Braid strips together; tuck ends under and seal. Place on greased cookie sheets. Cover; let rise in warm place until doubled in size, about 30 minutes. Heat oven to 375°F. Bake 25 to 35 minutes or until loaves sound hollow when lightly tapped. Immediately remove from cookie sheets; cool on wire racks.

2 WREATHS: Grease 2 cookie sheets. Divide dough into 6 parts. Remove air pockets by working dough with hands. On lightly floured surface, roll each to 24-inch rope. Braid 3 ropes together, stretching ropes while braiding to keep uniform in length. On greased cookie sheet, shape into ring; seal ends together. Repeat with remaining ropes. Cover; let rise in warm place until doubled in size, about 30 minutes. Heat oven to 375°F. Bake 25 to 35 minutes or until wreaths sound hollow when

Craft Gift Breads

lightly tapped. Immediately remove from cookie sheets; cool on wire racks.

To Preserve Bread:

Let loaves or wreaths dry in a cool, dry place for several days until very hard. (Large loaves require a week.) Brush or spray clear, glossy polyurethane or clear, glossy resin on all sides of bread. Let dry; repeat with second coat. If desired, more coats can be applied. The finished bread should have a clear, heavy sheen. When dry, decorate as desired.

To Decorate Bread:

LOAVES: Glue loaf to breadboard and decorate with a small sheaf of grain, dried berries, dried flowers, silk flowers or ribbon.

WREATHS: Attach a wire or ribbon for hanging. Make a ribbon or fabric bow; attach to wreath. Attach stalks of wheat, cinnamon sticks, pinecones, dried flowers or other holiday decorations.

Heart Baskets; Candy-Coated Pretzels

Candy-Coated Pretzels

8 ounces chocolate-flavored or vanilla-flavored candy coating

¼ teaspoon peppermint or mint extract, if desired

4 ounces small twist pretzels

½ cup crushed candy

Melt chocolate-flavored candy coating in medium saucepan over low heat, stirring constantly. Stir in peppermint extract. Place pan in hot water to maintain dipping consistency. Dip pretzels, entire or portion, into coating; allow excess to drip off. Place on waxed paper. Sprinkle dipped portion with crushed candy.

24 pretzels.

MICROWAVE DIRECTIONS: Place candy coating in small microwave-safe bowl. Microwave on HIGH for 1½ to 2 minutes or until smooth, stirring once halfway through cooking. Continue as directed above.

NUTRITION INFORMATION PER SERVING

Serving Size: 1 pretzel		Percent U.S. RDA	
Calories	80	Protein	*
Protein	1g	Vitamin A	*
Carbohydrate	12g	Vitamin C	*
Fat	3g	Thiamine	*
Cholesterol	2mg	Riboflavin	*
Sodium	90mg	Niacin	*
Potassium	35mg	Calcium	2%
		Iron	*
		*Contains less than 2%	

HOLIDAY TRIMMINGS

Holiday Hearts

Cut shapes as shown in Diagram 1 from 2 contrasting colors of paper. Mark and cut slits where indicated. Place 2 shapes at right angles to each other as shown in Diagram 2. Weave as follows:

Row 1 — Insert loop 1 into loop A, A into 2, 3 into A

Row 2 — Insert B into 1, 2 into B, B into 3

Row 3 — Insert 1 into C, C into 2, 3 into C

Adjust tension of weave so heart lies flat. If woven correctly, heart should open into a basket. Attach handle with paper glue. Fill with Candy-Coated Pretzels, assorted candies, nuts or cookies.

Diagram 1

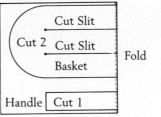

Diagram 2

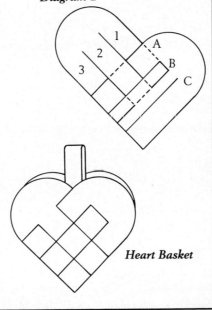

Heart Basket

Candy-Coated Pretzels

Include this perfect sweet-and-salty combination in a gift box of homemade candies.

Cherry Chip Cookie Wreaths

1 cup sugar
1 cup firmly packed brown sugar
1 cup margarine or butter, softened
1 cup oil
1 teaspoon vanilla
1 teaspoon almond extract
1 egg
3½ cups all purpose or unbleached flour
1 teaspoon baking soda
1 teaspoon cream of tartar
1 teaspoon salt
1 cup quick-cooking rolled oats
1 cup coconut
1 cup crisp rice cereal
1 cup miniature semi-sweet chocolate chips
½ cup maraschino cherries, chopped, drained on paper towels
Frosting tinted as desired
Assorted candies or candied cherries

Heat oven to 350°F. Line 2 large cookie sheets with foil. Grease outside of four 6-ounce (4-inch) custard cups; place 2 custard cups upside down on each cookie sheet. In large bowl, beat sugar, brown sugar and margarine until light and fluffy. Add oil, vanilla, almond extract and egg; beat well. Lightly spoon flour into measuring cup; level off. Add flour, baking soda, cream of tartar and salt; mix well. Stir in rolled oats, coconut, cereal and chocolate chips. Stir in cherries.* Press 1 cup dough around each custard cup, forming two 2-inch-wide wreaths on each cookie sheet.

Bake at 350°F. for 10 to 15 minutes or until light golden brown. Run knife around custard cups to loosen cookies. Carefully slide foil and cookie from each cookie sheet to wire rack. Cool completely. Remove custard cups; carefully remove foil from cookies. Re-line cooled cookie sheets with foil and repeat process with remaining dough. Decorate as desired with tinted frosting and assorted candies.**
8 wreaths; 8 servings each.

TIPS: *At this point, half of dough can be tightly covered and refrigerated for later baking. Bake within 3 days. For easier handling, let dough stand at room temperature 10 to 15 minutes before shaping.

**If tinted frosting is used, let frosting set and dry before storing. Store cookies flat, placing waxed paper between each cookie. Cover tightly and freeze for up to 1 month.

HIGH ALTITUDE—Above 3500 Feet: Decrease brown sugar to ½ cup and decrease oil to ½ cup. Bake as directed above.

NUTRITION INFORMATION PER SERVING

Serving Size: 1/64 of recipe		Percent U.S. RDA	
		Protein	*
Calories	140	Vitamin A	2%
Protein	1g	Vitamin C	*
Carbohydrate	17g	Thiamine	4%
Fat	8g	Riboflavin	2%
Cholesterol	3mg	Niacin	2%
Sodium	90mg	Calcium	*
Potassium	40mg	Iron	2%
		*Contains less than 2%	

Quick Spaghetti Sauce

Quick Spaghetti Sauce

1 pound ground beef
½ cup chopped onion
2 (15-ounce) cans tomato sauce
1 (4-ounce) can mushroom pieces
  and stems, drained
½ teaspoon oregano leaves
½ teaspoon basil leaves
¼ teaspoon garlic powder
⅛ to ¼ teaspoon cayenne pepper
⅛ teaspoon pepper

In large skillet or Dutch oven, brown ground beef and onion; drain. Add remaining ingredients; mix well. Simmer 15 minutes, stirring occasionally. Serve immediately over cooked spaghetti. Or cool slightly, ladle into clean jars, leaving ½-inch headspace. Cover with tight-fitting lids. Store in refrigerator.
10 (½-cup) servings.

MICROWAVE DIRECTIONS: In 2-quart microwave-safe casserole, crumble ground beef; add onion. Microwave on HIGH for 4 to 5 minutes or until meat is no longer pink, stirring once halfway through cooking; drain well. Add remaining ingredients; mix well. Microwave on HIGH for 8 to 10 minutes or until hot and flavors are blended.

NUTRITION INFORMATION PER SERVING

Serving Size: ½ cup		Percent U.S. RDA	
Calories	120	Protein	10%
Protein	9g	Vitamin A	15%
Carbohydrate	7g	Vitamin C	15%
Fat	6g	Thiamine	4%
Cholesterol	27mg	Riboflavin	6%
Sodium	570mg	Niacin	15%
Potassium	430mg	Calcium	2%
		Iron	8%

Quick Spaghetti Sauce

For the gadget lover on your gift list, accompany a gift of this sauce with a pasta server and pasta measure.

Chocolate Gingerbread Sleighs

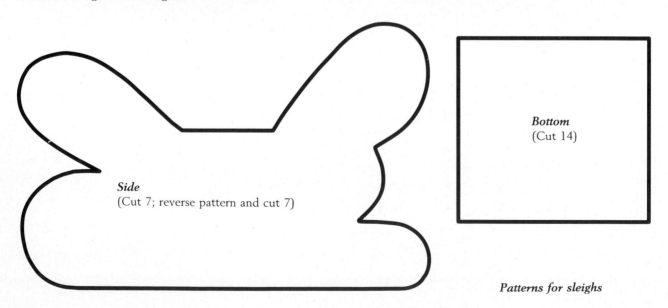

Side
(Cut 7; reverse pattern and cut 7)

Bottom
(Cut 14)

Patterns for sleighs

Chocolate Gingerbread Sleighs

⅔ cup firmly packed brown sugar
½ cup margarine or butter, softened
¼ cup molasses
1 egg yolk
1¾ cups all purpose or unbleached flour
2 tablespoons unsweetened cocoa
1 teaspoon baking soda
½ teaspoon salt
1½ teaspoons cinnamon
⅛ teaspoon ginger

FROSTING*
1 cup powdered sugar
¼ teaspoon cream of tartar
1 egg white

DECORATIONS
14 (3-inch) candy canes
Candy for decorations, if desired
Candy to fill sleigh

In large bowl, beat brown sugar and margarine until light and fluffy. Add molasses and egg yolk; blend well. Lightly spoon flour into measuring cup; level off. Add flour, cocoa, baking soda, salt, cinnamon and ginger; mix well. Cover with plastic wrap; refrigerate 2 hours for easier handling.

Trace pattern pieces and cut from heavy paper or light cardboard. Lightly grease cookie sheets. Heat oven to 350°F. On floured surface, roll half of dough to ³/₁₆-inch thickness. Refrigerate remaining dough. Using sleigh SIDE pattern, cut 7 sleigh SIDES; reserve trimmings. With large floured spatula, transfer pieces to greased cookie sheet, placing 1 inch apart. Turn pattern over; cut 7 additional sleigh SIDES. Place 1 inch apart on greased cookie sheet. Bake at 350°F. for 6 to 9 minutes or until set. Remove from cookie sheets; cool completely. Meanwhile, roll reserved trimmings to ³/₁₆-inch thickness. Using BOTTOM sleigh pattern, cut 14 BOTTOMS. Bake and cool as directed for sleigh SIDES.

In small bowl, beat all frosting ingredients at low speed until blended. Beat at high speed until stiff. Spoon frosting into decorating bag with medium writing tip. (Keep any remaining frosting covered with damp paper towel or plastic wrap.)

To assemble sleighs, place 1 sleigh SIDE, back side up, on flat surface. Pipe frosting along 1 edge of each of 2 BOTTOMS. Attach BOTTOMS to sleigh SIDE as shown by dotted line on diagram. Pipe frosting along top edges of BOTTOMS. Attach second sleigh SIDE, front side up, on BOTTOMS, making sure both sleigh SIDES are even. Hold in place a few seconds until frosting is set. Repeat with remaining sleigh SIDES and BOTTOMS to make 7 sleighs. Wrap decorating bag in plastic wrap to keep from drying out. Let sleighs stand 1 hour or until frosting is completely dry.

To decorate, using frosting in decorating bag, attach a candy cane along outside bottom edges of each sleigh to resemble runners. Using small writing tip, write name on each side of sleigh. Decorate with frosting and candies, as desired. To serve, fill sleighs with candies.

7 sleighs.

TIP: *We are using this recipe for frosting even though it contains raw egg whites. It sets up quickly, dries very hard, and keeps well. There is a possibility of raw eggs being contaminated with salmonella. Therefore, we do not recommend that this be eaten. If the sleighs are apt to be eaten, substitute ready-to-spread frosting.

HIGH ALTITUDE — Above 3500 Feet: No change.

Chocolate Gingerbread Sleighs

Fill these sleighs with assorted candies and use them as place cards or festive personalized gifts.

Placement of bottom squares for assembling sleighs

Holiday Muffin Mix

Holiday Muffin Mix

An easy gift to prepare, this recipe yields enough mix for four recipes of Holiday Muffins.

5 cups all purpose or unbleached flour
1 cup whole wheat flour
1½ cups sugar
1 cup instant nonfat dry milk
¼ cup baking powder
2 teaspoons salt
1 tablespoon cinnamon
½ teaspoon cloves

Lightly spoon flour into measuring cup; level off. In large bowl, combine all ingredients; blend well. Store in airtight container at room temperature or in cool dry place. For gift giving, measure 2 cups mix (by dipping cup into mix and leveling off) and place in airtight container or zipper-topped storage bag. Be sure to include recipe for Holiday Muffins.

About 8 cups mix.

HIGH ALTITUDE—Above 3500 Feet: Decrease baking powder to 2½ tablespoons.

Holiday Muffins

2 cups Holiday Muffin Mix
⅔ cup water
1 egg, slightly beaten
¼ cup oil

Heat oven to 400°F. Grease bottoms only of 12 muffin cups or line with paper baking cups. Place muffin mix in medium bowl. Add water, egg and oil; stir until dry ingredients are just moistened. *Do not overmix.* Fill greased muffin cups approximately ½ full. Bake at 400°F. for 10 to 15 minutes or until toothpick inserted in center comes out clean. Immediately remove from pan. Serve warm.

12 muffins.

MICROWAVE DIRECTIONS: Using a 6-cup microwave-safe muffin pan, line each cup with 2 paper baking cups to absorb moisture during baking. Prepare muffin batter as directed above. Fill muffin cups ½ full. Microwave on HIGH for 1¾ to 2¼ minutes or until toothpick inserted in center comes out clean. *Rotate pan ½ turn halfway through baking.* Remove muffins from pan and immediately discard outer baking cups. Cool 1 minute on wire rack before serving. Repeat with remaining batter.

TIP: One-half cup miniature chocolate chips or ½ cup pecan pieces can be added to batter.

HIGH ALTITUDE—Above 3500 Feet: Bake at 425°F. for 10 to 15 minutes.

NUTRITION INFORMATION PER SERVING

Serving Size: 1 muffin		Percent U.S. RDA	
Calories	140	Protein	4%
Protein	3g	Vitamin A	*
Carbohydrate	19g	Vitamin C	*
Fat	5g	Thiamine	8%
Cholesterol	18mg	Riboflavin	6%
Sodium	180mg	Niacin	4%
Potassium	70mg	Calcium	8%
		Iron	4%
		*Contains less than 2%	

Pictured left to right: Berry Rosé Jelly; Holiday Muffin Mix

Berry Rosé Jelly

3½ cups sugar
1½ cups raspberry-cranberry drink
⅛ teaspoon cinnamon
⅛ teaspoon cloves
½ cup rosé wine
1 (3-ounce) package liquid fruit pectin

In large saucepan, combine sugar, raspberry-cranberry drink, cinnamon and cloves. Bring to a full rolling boil, stirring to dissolve sugar. Boil 1 minute, stirring constantly. Remove from heat; stir in wine and pectin. Skim foam. Ladle into clean, hot 8-ounce jelly jars or moisture- and vaporproof freezer containers, leaving ½-inch headspace. Cool slightly; cover with tight-fitting lids. Let stand several hours at room temperature or until set. Store in refrigerator up to 3 weeks or in freezer up to 3 months. 3¾ cups.

NUTRITION INFORMATION PER SERVING

Serving Size: 1 tablespoon		Percent U.S. RDA	
Calories	50	Protein	*
		Vitamin A	*
Protein	0g	Vitamin C	2%
Carbohydrate	13g	Thiamine	*
Fat	0g	Riboflavin	*
Cholesterol	0mg	Niacin	*
Sodium	0mg	Calcium	*
Potassium	5mg	Iron	*
		*Contains less than 2%	

Berry Rosé Jelly

Rosé wine adds a wonderful flavor to this sparkling jelly. Serve it with Holiday Muffins for a sensational breakfast treat.

Appendix

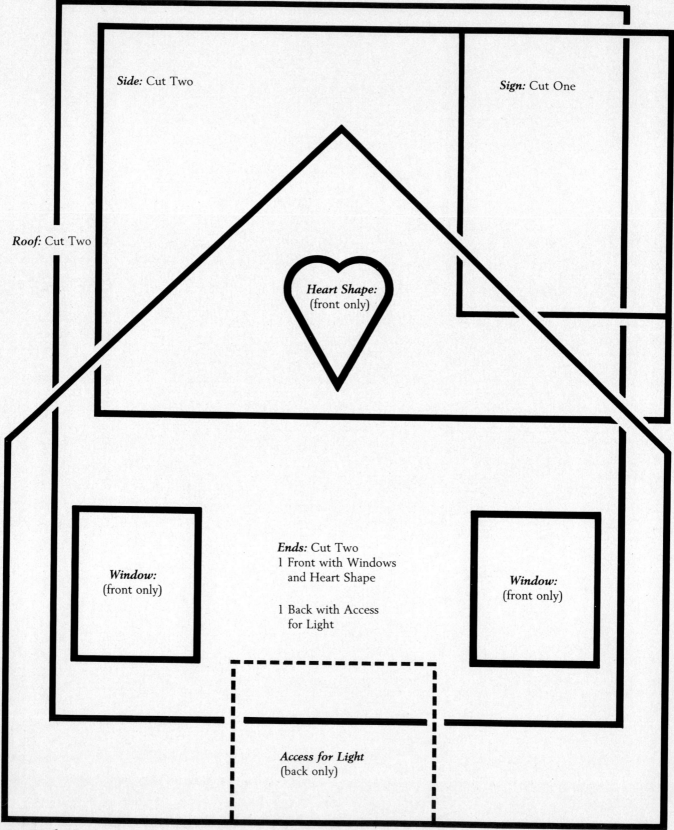

Side: Cut Two

Sign: Cut One

Roof: Cut Two

Heart Shape:
(front only)

Window:
(front only)

Ends: Cut Two
1 Front with Windows
and Heart Shape

1 Back with Access
for Light

Window:
(front only)

Access for Light
(back only)

Patterns for Santa's Gingerbread Bake Shoppe (see recipe page 88)

Nutrition Information

Nutrition Information: Pillsbury recipe analysis is provided per serving or per unit of food and is based on the most current nutritional values available from the United States Department of Agriculture (USDA) and food manufacturers. Each recipe is calculated for number of calories; grams of protein, carbohydrate and fat; and milligrams of cholesterol, sodium and potassium.

Vitamin and mineral levels are stated as percentages of United States Recommended Daily Allowances. RDAs are the dietary standards determined by the U.S. Food and Drug Administration for healthy people. If you are following a medically prescribed diet, consult your physician or registered dietitian about using this nutrition information.

Calculating Nutrition Information: Recipe analysis is calculated on:

· A single serving based on the largest number of servings, or on a specific amount (1 tablespoon) or unit (1 cookie).

· The first ingredient or amount when more than one is listed.

· "If desired" or garnishing ingredients when they are included in the ingredient listing.

· Only the amount of a marinade or frying oil absorbed during preparation.

Using Nutrition Information: The amount of nutrients a person needs is determined by one's age, size and activity level. The following are general guidelines you can use for evaluating your daily food intake:

Calories: 2,350
Protein: 45 to 65 grams
Carbohydrates: 340 grams
Fat: 80 grams or less
Cholesterol: 300 milligrams or less
Sodium: 2,400 milligrams

A nutritionally balanced diet recommends limiting intake of fat to 30 percent or less of total daily calories. One gram of fat is 9 calories. You can determine the fat content of recipes or products with the following formula:

$$\frac{\text{GRAMS OF FAT PER SERVING} \times 9}{\text{TOTAL CALORIES PER SERVING}} = \frac{\text{PERCENT}}{\text{OF CALORIES}} \text{ FROM FAT}$$

$$\left(\text{Ex. } \frac{8 \times 9}{310} = \frac{72}{310} = 22\%\right)$$

Pillsbury Products Used in Recipes

DRY GROCERY PRODUCTS:

Canned Vegetables
Green Giant® Mushrooms Pieces and Stems
Green Giant® Sliced Mushrooms

Flour
Pillsbury's BEST® All Purpose Flour
Pillsbury's BEST® Unbleached All Purpose Flour
Pillsbury's BEST® Whole Wheat Flour

Frosting
Pillsbury Chocolate Fudge Frosting Supreme™
Pillsbury Coconut Pecan Frosting Supreme™
Pillsbury Cream Cheese Frosting Supreme™
Pillsbury Vanilla Frosting Supreme™

Mixes
Breads
Pillsbury Hot Roll Mix
Pillsbury Cranberry Quick Bread Mix
Pillsbury Date Quick Bread Mix
Pillsbury Nut Quick Bread Mix
Cake
Pillsbury Plus® Butter Recipe Cake Mix
Pillsbury Plus® Devil's Food Cake Mix

Specialty Products
Hungry Jack® Mashed Potato Flakes
Hungry Jack® Syrup

REFRIGERATED PRODUCTS:

Pillsbury's BEST® Refrigerated Sugar Cookies
Pillsbury Refrigerated Quick Crescent Dinner Rolls
Pillsbury Refrigerated Soft Breadsticks
Pillsbury All Ready Pie Crusts

FROZEN PRODUCTS:

Green Giant® American Mixtures™
Heartland Style Broccoli, Cauliflower and Carrots

Index